SUSTAINABLY DELICIOUS

MAKING *the* WORLD *a* BETTER PLACE, ONE RECIPE *at a* TIME

MICHEL NISCHAN

with MARY GOODBODY

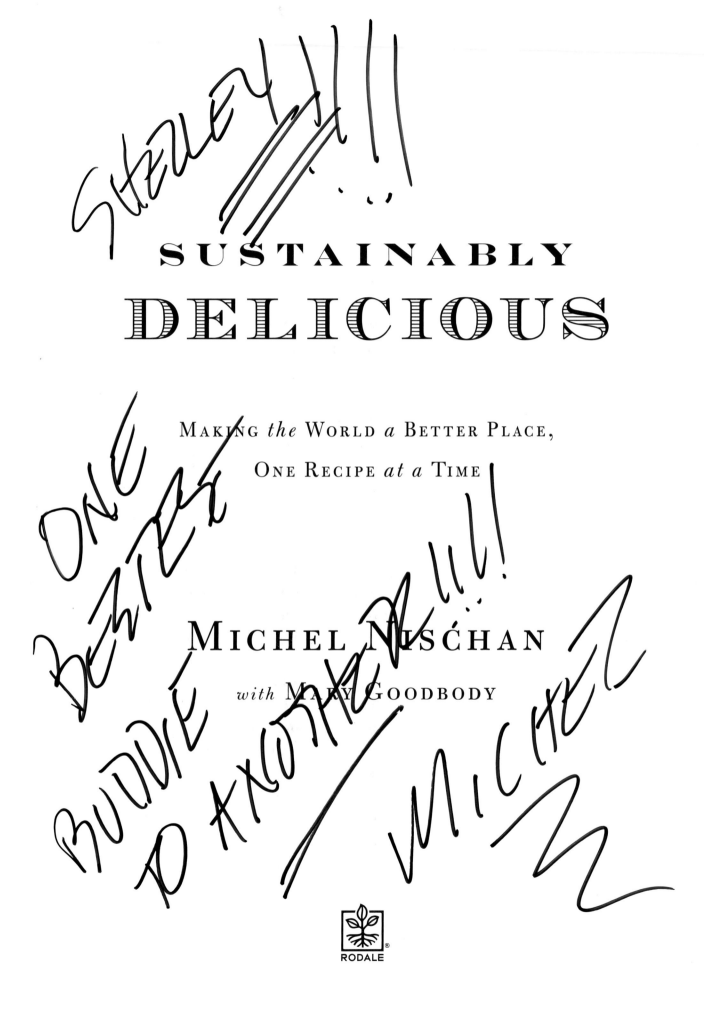

RODALE

Rodale books may be purchased for business or promotional use or for special sales.
For information, please write to:Special Markets Department,
Rodale Inc., 733 Third Avenue, New York, NY 10017.

Printed in the United States of America
Rodale Inc. makes every effort to use acid-free ∞, recycled paper ♲.

Book design by Christopher Rhoads

Library of Congress Cataloging-in-Publication Data

Nischan, Michel.
    Sustainably delicious : making the world a better place, one recipe at a time / by Michel Nischan
with Mary Goodbody.
        p.   cm.
    Includes bibliographical references and index.
    ISBN-13: 978-1-60529-998-3 (hardcover)
    ISBN-10: 1-60529-998-7 (hardcover)
    1. Cookery (Natural foods)   2. Natural foods.   3. Sustainable living.   I. Goodbody, Mary. II. Title.
TX741.N58 2010
641.5'636—dc22

                                                                                2009029222

Distributed to the trade by Macmillan

2   4   6   8   10   9   7   5   3   1   hardcover

We inspire and enable people to improve their lives and the world around them
For more of our products visit **rodalestore.com** or call 800-848-4735

In memory of John Mohawk of the Seneca Nation for his work to preserve and raise awareness of the nearly extinct Iroquois white corn, which has been so important to the health of his land, his culture, his community, and his ancestry. He is now one of the many kernels in the night sky. I am sure other great visionaries like Terrol Dew Johnson will continue with the same passion and dedication, as tepary beans are equally delicious and important.

Contents

FOREWORD

Foodies, as those of us whose lives are entangled in the web of food from the garden to the kitchen affectionately call ourselves, are passionately interested in what we put on our tables. We can't resist the lure of new flavors, of a unique preparation, but we also prize the simple joy of a tried-and-true meal lovingly prepared for friends and family. We love the tastes, the spices, and the sweet, salt, and sour. We love exploring the subtle changes a dash of vinegar imparts to a dish or trying a new recipe for the black cod we picked up from our local fisherman at the farmers' market. We enjoy searching for ingredients, the proverbial hunting and gathering from markets and our gardens. Growing vegetables and fruits and, for some, raising poultry or fishing; preparing and eating food; and incessant talking about food—these are the favored pursuits of any self-respecting Foodie. Not only do we find these tasks enjoyable, they are an essential part of our life fabric, and we embrace them!

Occasionally, I meet someone, like Michel, who takes these pursuits to exceptional lengths. Michel is unique among the Foodies as one whose passions extend well beyond the table, beyond the kitchen. Michel could perhaps more appropriately be described as a food activist, a tireless representative of the silent soil. He gives the farmer who isn't heard at the dinner table a voice, and he has his eye on a story bigger than the next menu. Michel, humble Michel, would probably not describe himself as a steward of these things, but knowing him as I do, I've come to appreciate how these principles subtly illuminate his work. He has woven together the beautiful collection of recipes you hold in your hands—pages that unfold not just as a guide to cooking wonderful food, but that reveal the essential wisdom of how our food choices impact the world around us. It is one thing to cook delicious food, and quite another to extend the culinary art into the fabric of your life and the lives of those around you. This is Michel's true gift.

When my father established Dressing Room, his opening act as a restaurateur, it marked a turning point in our food relationship. For years I had been whispering, or rather shouting, in my father's ear about the link between organic agriculture and the environment. Trying to speak his language, I'd often resort to theater metaphor to make my point: "Pop, you always say that making a movie without a good script leaves all the actors chewing on the props. Well, just as a good script is the foundation of a good movie, organic agriculture is the screenplay for good food, happy farmers, a healthy planet. And, most importantly, it's how you get the best tomatoes to serve with your hamburger at Dressing Room!" (A good hamburger was very important to my father!)

As it turned out, my father was already with me on this one and was looking for someone to bring this philosophy to life in the kitchen of Dressing Room. "Pop," I said to him, "you have to meet Michel Nischan. I think he's going to play the starring role in your restaurant project."

And so it came to pass that Westport, Connecticut, was treated to Michel's exceptional cuisine, and the farmers of New England were given an extraordinary showcase for the organic fruits of their labors. In keeping with his preference for organic, local, and sustainable ingredients, Michel decided early on to purchase almost exclusively from local purveyors. In doing so, he gave local economies a boost, reestablishing traditions that hundreds of years ago were common in Connecticut and throughout New England. Westport and the surrounding areas were heavily farmed before they became the bedroom communities they are today. I spent much of my childhood in the fields just behind what is now Dressing Room. The nearby streams are where I learned to fish, and I remember chickens running across the roads very close to what is now downtown Westport. The menu Michel orchestrated at Dressing Room started a very special process of rebirth for these long dormant fields and farm, a very personal one for me, and my childhood neighborhood.

Sustainably Delicious, the wonderful book before you, may be one of Michel's finest acts. Flip through the pages and see the gorgeous images of fresh vegetables dancing on the pages. Let Michel's recipes guide you to new tastes or encourage you to experiment with an ingredient you have never before prepared. (The sweet pea with lemon ricotta ravioli is something I can't wait to try when my peas are ripe!) When you bring this lovely book into your kitchen and read the thoughtful and poignant words, remember that by preparing his food you are helping Michel spread his message and becoming part of what could be the most important movement in our lifetime: shifting the economy toward a sustainable future. Join me and Michel on this journey. Experience how the simple act of preparing organic food can have a powerful effect on the world around you.

PS: Do you know where your food comes from?

Nell Newman
Backyard farmer and Foodie

INTRODUCTION

Anyone who takes the time to shop and cook from scratch starts off wanting to make good food choices, but with terms like *sustainable, organic,* and *locavore* being tossed around so freely, many home cooks are confused about how best to feed their families. Which foods are organic? Why should we buy locally grown produce? What is grass-fed beef and why should we care, let alone pay more for it?

With *Sustainably Delicious,* I address these and other issues with recipes and advice for cooking sensibly by celebrating the dishes and techniques that once defined us as a nation of great cooks. When we choose local and sustainably grown foods, we are rewarded with the very best flavors nature is capable of producing. Just consider the difference between a vine-ripened heirloom tomato at its peak in August and one of those "on the vine" tomatoes you find in the produce section in February. You probably know how much better the local tomato tastes; what you might not know is how much better that tomato is for you and the environment. What I've come to realize after more than 25 years of hands-on involvement in the sustainable-food movement is simply this: Where there is flavor, there are nutrients, and where there are nutrients, there is health.

This doesn't mean I'm not sympathetic to budgetary concerns—we all have them. Just know that you can find amazing local produce, meats, fish, and other products without breaking the bank or traveling hither and yon if you begin one step at a time and accept that it will be something of an adventure. Once you get into it, you will find that buying even a few things that are grown locally and/or organically is a major improvement over buying none. You will be making a difference environmentally, and yet you will not blow your weekly food budget. I know this is so because although I am a restaurant chef by trade, my wife, Lori, and I have five kids: Lauren, Courtney, Chris, Drew, and Ethan. My interest in sustainable home cooking while balancing a food budget is not only genuine, it's also necessary!

I believe wholeheartedly in sustainability, so it's no surprise it defines how I cook and how I live. It means eating foods produced on farms and from orchards that apply no added chemical fertilizers and pesticides and that employ the sorts of sensible farming practices that nurture the soil for future generations of crops as well as people. It means knowing which fish are in danger of being overfished and which are okay to eat—fish like blackfish (also known as tautog) and wild Alaskan salmon are great choices; red snapper and swordfish are not. It means understanding that responsible animal husbandry is not only more humane for the livestock, it is also better for the land because it restores and maintains pasture health, reduces pollution caused by excessively concentrated waste, and does not depend on massive amounts of grains grown on conventional (i.e., chemically assisted) monoculture, corporate farms.

There's another benefit to eating grass-fed or pasture-raised meat (the two terms are pretty much synonymous) that I was excited to learn: Pasture-raised animals possess omega-3 fatty acids—fatty acids that until recently were thought to exist only in fish and a few plants and are crucial for brain function and normal development, as well as protection against cardiac disease. The American Heart Association recommends eating foods rich in omega-3s at least twice a week.

There is more to eating sustainably. It also means eating from a wide range of available foods in their season. In my kitchen and I hope in yours, this results in pure excitement when we work with fruits and vegetables we may not know a lot about, such as heirloom apples, kohlrabi, and quince. We also should cook with lesser-known or less popular cuts of meat (a steer is not made up of steaks alone!) and investigate foods that may be unfamiliar, such as ancient grains or pullet eggs.

Eating this way helps support the health of the planet, but it's also good for the health of our families, both physically and spiritually. Eating sustainably means cooking from scratch; starting with fresh produce whenever we can; and adding sensible amounts of animal fats, unrefined sweeteners, and salt to our dishes, relying instead on the quality and integrity of carefully grown ingredients combined with time-honored cooking methods to bring out the best flavors.

Equally important, it means working and cooking together so that one person isn't doing it all. A recurring theme in this book is how joyful it can be to include your kids in the kitchen and how much more they will anticipate meals if they have had a hand in getting them on the table.

When we cook this way, we know exactly what is in the food we put on the table, as well as where it came from and often who grew it. This is food that encourages families to gather for truly meaningful interactions at mealtimes. This is food that comes with countless stories that can be shared along with fond memories of growing, congregating, cooking, or all of the above.

You will notice that there are no recipes for desserts in *Sustainably Delicious.* I know how much folks like a sweet at the end of the meal, but I decided to forgo them here for two reasons. First, I enjoy fresh, sweet fruit far more than any sugary cake or cookie, and I nearly always finish a meal with plump berries or juicy, ripe peaches, pears, or apples. Second, and more pertinent, two of our children are diabetic, so Lori and I have long banished most sweets from the house—and everyone does just fine. As I could produce only a finite number of recipes, I decided to fill the following pages with the recipes I cook and eat all the time.

Paul Newman, Dressing Room, and Me

I've spent a good deal of my life working with food and with farmers. Being a chef born of farmers, it is easy for me to understand the direct connection between the food I cook and where it comes from. When I first began cooking and buying (I admit, in the early days it was primarily trying to buy) from farmers, I did so because it seemed to be common sense. Why cook something if you're not sure who grew it or how it was treated? As I continued to search for farmers who could supply me, information slowly and surely began to percolate publicly toward an awareness of how our food choices impact the environment, our personal health, and the health of our communities. Common sense turned into cause, and cause turned into broader action.

Along the way, I was privileged to meet others who felt as I did. One of the most remarkable meetings—and most germane to this book—was being introduced to Nell Newman by Greg Higgins, a mutual friend. Both Nell and Greg were active in the sustainability movement, Greg as the owner of Higgins Restaurant in Portland, Oregon, and Nell as a passionate advocate and organic-food producer. Nell called one day to explain that her "pop" wanted to open a restaurant in Connecticut. She asked if I would be willing to help her father to ensure that the Newman family values would be addressed. These values included supporting local producers, organics, and sustainability. My admiration for Nell and her work was well established, even without having met her face-to-face, so when I met her in person, how could I possibly say no? I next was introduced to Paul Newman.

I have never been a movie buff, so I was not a major fan. I had only seen *Butch Cassidy and the Sundance Kid* and *The Verdict*—both great films, to be sure, but not significant on my radar. I did have intense respect for Paul's very blatant style of über-philanthropy. For someone to give away every penny of more than $200 million (and by now far more) in food-business profits was, to my way of thinking, very Mother Teresa (for a guy) and very Dalai Lama (for a beer-drinking race-car driver). Paul had three special fingers: On one he wore his wedding ring, and on another his Formula One ring; the third was directed at the IRS and wasteful government spending. He wanted the profits from the good fortune of Newman's Own to bypass governmental red tape and go straight to the many who needed it most. This, to me, is what made Newman a very cool guy.

Something else that quadrupled the "cool factor" was that he and I liked a lot of the same types of food: meat loaf, oysters, great burgers, corned-beef sandwiches, and beer. I'll never forget his amazement at my ability to eat a gigantic hamburger without it falling apart. I showed him my "pinch and push" method one day at a local Westport, Connecticut, restaurant called Mario's, where the burgers are truly immense. He was astounded and impressed. We became friends.

As time went on, Paul and I crafted real-time solutions for opening Dressing Room, a locally supplied restaurant in a state that loses more than 6,000 acres of farmland per year. One solution was to open a farmers' market in the restaurant's parking lot. Our weekly local produce from more than 20 farmers would be delivered right to our doorstep, and our neighbors in surrounding communities could benefit at the same time.

We designed the market to be producer only, no middlemen, which made it special. At the time there were only a couple of similar markets in Connecticut, run by City Seed of New Haven. The vast majority of the other "farmers' markets" resold produce imported from California, Florida, and other faraway places. Our model provided multiple benefits and was enthusiastically received by pretty much everyone.

Once Dressing Room and the weekly farmers' market opened and customers for both voiced their enthusiastic support of our dedication to American food and local farmers, we longed to make the kind of food we were buying and cooking available to everyone—especially those who could not afford it. Wholesome Wave Foundation was born to encourage farmers' markets and farm stands to open smack-dab in the middle of underserved and forgotten communities that crave access to pure, fresh food. Innovations such as doubling the value of food stamps and WIC (Women, Infants, and Children) hunger-relief benefits were initiated through Wholesome Wave and succeeded in large part because of the ever-infectious goodness of Paul's generosity.

When I think of Paul, what always comes back to me—and what I miss most—is his honest curiosity, coupled with an open, if stubborn, mind regarding organics and sustainability.

He also possessed an uncanny ability to understand what people want to eat. For example, he was so fond of black cod that he wanted it on the menu all the time. When I explained that between poor fishery management and overpopularity, the noble cod faces a one-two punch for survival—which meant that hook-and-line-caught Chatham Cod was the only sustainable choice we could make and then only during a few months, at best—he said, "Damn. I guess I'll be eating less cod." And his comments about pickles not having enough "boing!" or the cheese on the burger not being tangy enough were always dead-on.

Although Paul did not instill my beliefs regarding local, regional, sustainable, and artisanal foods—they have always been a deep part of me—how he embraced our venture and encouraged our work had a profound and unexpected effect on me and everyone involved with Dressing Room. He ignited an intense desire within me to spread the word, the reach, and the depth of this vital and generous gospel. Not because it is righteous or noble, but simply because it is right—period.

He will be forever missed.

SUSTAINABLE YOU

We constantly have to weigh our decisions and determine if they support a brighter future for ourselves, our children, and our world.

For anyone on this personal journey to sustainability, I have some advice: Start with one step. Only you know what you can afford, what you are willing to do or not do, and what you can tackle without feeling beleaguered. This might mean buying some organic produce at the supermarket, using the same coffee cup all day long, or refilling aluminum bottles with tap water instead of relying on bottled water. It might mean taking canvas bags to the market or recycling the plastic ones you have collected over the months and years. It might mean enlisting the kids' help in the kitchen or talking with them about ways you can "save the earth" as a family.

You might think it's insignificant if you replace just two items on your shopping list with organic products—say, milk and apples. How much of a difference does that actually make? And yet, can you imagine what would happen if 30 or 40 percent of American households bought only organic milk and apples? Two industries would change dramatically. Don't think otherwise: You can be a sustainability hero one choice at a time.

The great thing is that once you take the first step, you will feel good about it, and you can take another step, and another. Twenty-five years ago, when I first entered the movement, I never thought the day would come when most supermarkets carried organic produce and had whole sections devoted to natural foods. I never dreamed that most public places, including restaurants, would be smoke free. I certainly never expected to see such a growth in farmers' markets. In fact, the farmers' market movement is growing so rapidly that there are not enough farmers to keep up with demand. A "good problem," to be sure, but also a troubling one. *Are we running out of farmers?* We can all help by getting to know who the local farmers and suppliers are and then supporting them. One way to do this is to make a point of buying and cooking ingredients that may not appeal to you at first—foods such as black barley and celery root. In

my recipes, I use these ingredients and more, and while I offer substitutes when appropriate, I hope you try them; I want you to discover the glory of these and so many other humble foods.

As a restaurant chef, I have sought out farms to supply Dressing Room's kitchen with the best the state of Connecticut has to offer. One of my favorites is Millstone Farm, which is a good example of a small farm well worth supporting. We buy organic lettuces and vegetables through Annie Farrell from Betsy and Jesse Fink's 75-acre farm, which they run as a closed-loop, sustainable operation. This means they make every effort to farm their land as a holistic system, never bringing inputs for the soil onto the property from elsewhere but instead relying on amending and caring for the land with cover crops and farm-animal manure. As they say on their Web site, www.millstonefarm.org, "We believe that we can make a better future by helping people simplify the way we make the food that ends up running our bodies. We believe we take a risk when our food supply is completely out of our own hands. Science is helping us better understand those risks, from disease to deforestation to a lower and lower quality of nutrient value in our meals."

Millstone Farm stands as a pioneering model for other regional farms. It's worth it to look for a farm in your area that follows this paradigm so that you can have locally grown greens and vegetables most of the year. And as you read and cook from *Sustainably Delicious,* you will join me in a delicious, nourishing, and neighborly journey to a new, sustainable you.

SUSTAINABLE SHOPPING

As cool as it is to shop at farmers' markets, I know that for many of us it's not always possible. When it is, though, embrace it with enthusiasm. If you don't know where the nearest farmers' market is, go to www.localharvest.org to discover a few in your region. The key is to look for things you usually buy at the supermarket and instead buy them at the farm stand. These may include lettuces, apples, tomatoes, berries, jams, pickles, eggs, and cheese. Many farmers' markets also offer locally baked bread and farm-raised meat. A word of warning: When you walk through a farmers' market, you will be tempted to buy more than you might actually need. My advice? Bring a list or know beforehand what you want to cook. I know this plan may change on a dime (who can resist those new potatoes or freshly laid eggs?), but it's worth considering and really does help keep costs (and waste) in check.

Most American families cannot live by farmers' markets alone, so we need to supplement our outings with forays to the supermarket. If you can, buy the organic produce offered by most chains these days, as well as organic milk, whole grain cereals, and multigrain breads. Look for products that are not overpackaged and that use postconsumer paper and cardboard for their packaging. Avoid those "free" plastic bags from the produce section, too, if you can. Much produce, from apples to potatoes, should not be stored in plastic (and will be peeled or washed before use), so why transport it home that way?

If there is one behavior you change, let it be breaking the bottled water habit. Please. According to Earth Policy Institute, bottled water "can cost up to 10,000 times more than tap water. At as much as $2.50 per liter ($10 per gallon), bottled water costs more than gasoline." How is that beneficial to the planet? Tap water in most municipalities is very good, but if you don't like the flavor, buy a filter for the tap or a pitcher with a filter. Fill reusable bottles and take them with you. I promise, you won't miss bottled water at all (and your weekly grocery bill will shrink a little).

THE SUSTAINABLE KITCHEN

Part of sustainability is developing sensible habits in the kitchen. I urge you to compost and recycle as much as you can. Most nonprotein food scraps can go in the compost, which you can maintain near your garden or at the back of your yard. Add kitchen refuse to yard clippings and garden trimmings, and before long you will have rich, dark compost to mix with the soil. Healthy soil equals healthy plants, and that's a very good thing.

Recycle everything your town accepts. This might include paper, glass, aluminum, and plastic, as well as thin cardboard such as that used for boxes holding cereal, pasta, and rice.

Cut down on paper products. A dish towel works just as well as a few sheets of paper towel to wipe up spills. Producing and recycling paper towels and napkins takes more energy than is used when you toss their cloth counterparts into the laundry with your other items. Lori and I have pretty much abandoned conventional cleaning products in favor of natural ones. While I don't tend to get overly concerned about bacteria in the kitchen, when you wipe the counters and stove top with a clean sponge or rag and some vinegar mixed with lemon juice, you will kill most anything that lurks.

To save water, don't leave the tap running while you tidy up the kitchen. Run the dishwasher when it's full, and rinse off lightly used glasses and plates in the sink and let them drain dry for later use.

Vacuum the refrigerator coils several times a year, and keep the refrigerator and freezer compartments well stocked but not jam-packed. Chilled food keeps the other food cold; an overloaded or understocked refrigerator only makes the appliance work harder as air circulation is either restricted or too free. While a freezer does best packed a little tighter than a refrigerator, it should not be stuffed to overflowing.

Make sure you have good light in the kitchen where you need it. If the windows are covered with curtains or blinds, consider removing them and letting the sun shine in. Replace incandescent bulbs with fluorescent ones, which live longer and are far less expensive to operate.

If you like to cook, spending time in the kitchen is a joy. In cold weather, the room is warm and cozy, with something good in the oven or simmering on the back burner releasing a heady, comforting aroma. In the summer, colorful vegetables and fruit fill bowls and baskets, and just thinking about preparing them is enough to make our mouths water and our creativity percolate. With the refrigerator humming, the oven blasting heat, and water running freely in the sink, it's easy to see how the act of cooking can ratchet up utility bills and sabotage our good intentions. It does not have to be this way if we take a few commonsense measures.

✤ Plan to cook what you buy. How often have you found wilted herbs, flabby broccoli, or mushy apples in the refrigerator? Or how about chicken parts coated with frost and freezer burned in the back of the freezer? Remember what's in there, or post a list if you need a reminder. Have a plan and stick to it. Eat what you buy soon after purchase, or freeze it and keep a log so that you eat from the freezer with a sensible strategy.

- Use water wisely. Fill the sink when you clean vegetables rather than running them under cold water. When cooking, fill the sink or a plastic tub with just enough warm, soapy water to cover used cooking utensils. When done, all you need to do is rinse them and let them dry.

- Use the stove correctly. If your oven requires preheating, know how long it takes to reach a desired temperature. If a recipe says to "preheat the oven to 350°F," don't turn on the oven until you are ready. I try to put the preheat instructions in a sensible place in the recipe, but you may not work as quickly as I do, or your oven may heat up in 5 minutes while mine takes 15. Be aware.

  Don't leave the burners on when you are not using them. Be conscious of the heat intensity needed for a cooking method, and turn the heat up or down accordingly. When you cook anything that needs to be brought to a simmer, put the lid on the pot (unless specifically instructed not to). This speeds up the process and saves energy.

- Use leftovers. Somehow, leftovers have gotten a bad rap. They are considered second-class citizens instead of opportunities for the broad-minded, inspired cook. Less energy is required to reheat leftovers than to cook something new from scratch, and often leftovers need no reheating at all. I love to spread the celery root puree on page 210 on bread to moisten sandwiches, and I use leftover pork chops to make hash. Soups are a great way to use leftover vegetables, which also can be tossed with pasta or grains for a simple meal. Use your imagination and turn leftovers into treasures.

THE SUSTAINABLE FAMILY

I say this often, but it's true: In my experience, when my kids help in the garden or the kitchen, they are far more inclined to try new foods and unfamiliar dishes. My youngest son, Ethan, who is diabetic, discovered how amazing and sweet young carrots pulled directly from the earth taste. Although I lost some of my crop to his enthusiasm, I was thrilled that he was opting for carrots over the occasional sugar-free ice pop. My oldest son, Chris, complains about having to turn the compost during the summer, but I have heard him explaining to his friends how much it helps the soil and how good the food from our garden tastes.

Bring this same philosophy into the kitchen. Get the kids to help you, and set aside time on a weekend morning or afternoon. Divide and conquer and see how much food gets prepped for the week to come. These can be happy hours spent working together. The kids will grumble in the beginning, I guarantee, but in the end they won't mind much. Talking and joking while you work is easy, and you might be surprised at how much fun you end up having. When it's time for supper, everyone will be eager to taste the fruits of their labor (pun intended).

Working together to live more sustainably extends outside the kitchen, too. I always say two adults, three kids, and five rakes saves money and gas on lawn guys and leaf blowers. Get rid of one of the cars or determine not to use it as much; the family that rides together reduces its carbon footprint together. Look for some of the great television documentaries on saving the planet or living gently on the earth, and watch them as a family. Once the kids get hooked on the concept, they will find numerous and interesting ways to extend it. And they won't refrain from keeping you in line!

The Sustainable Community

We have a large vegetable garden in our suburban backyard. Lori and I started it several years ago to give our kids some of the same experiences I had growing up. When I was a kid, my mom, who grew up on a farm, tended a backyard garden that was so expansive it took over the entire yard. As I like to say, the garden came right up to the sliding glass door of our suburban Illinois home, leaving no room for swing sets or lawn furniture. From working in that garden and eating from it, I learned a lot about sustainability without ever realizing it.

Although I love the produce we get from our garden, what I enjoy even more is the way it attracts our next-door neighbors, our back-door neighbors, our across-the-street neighbors, and our across-town neighbors. Ours is not the only garden on our street. My next-door neighbor Bob grows strawberries and blueberries, and, just as I welcome him to my garden, he welcomes us with our berry-collecting buckets.

I built a large table for the garden, perfect for organizing our harvest and also for hosting outdoor meals. I dug a fire pit at the top of the garden and lined it with some of the oversize Connecticut rocks I pulled from the land when I was preparing the beds. Everyone likes to gather in the garden: our family, our kids' buddies, neighbors, dear friends, and new acquaintances. Some people help with the garden, others prepare food picked from it, and still others provide entertainment. Everyone has a good time. Eating on and from the land harks back to earlier times. It's a reinvention of the old-fashioned block parties and village picnics that used to characterize America's small towns and close-knit communities when every household boasted a famous pie or chicken-with-dumplings recipe.

These communities were self-sustaining, with the farmers supplying the food and the townspeople the commerce. I am not suggesting we go back to those times (if ever we could!), but I am suggesting we all seek more community. When you feed your neighbors, you make a connection that is irreplaceable. Plus, it can easily open a dialogue about food and sustainability: "I got these asparagus at the farmers' market. Do you want to come with me next week?"

When we see a friend in the supermarket aisle, we nod and smile and wheel our carts rapidly away. Who has time to stop and chat? When we shop at the grocery store, we are on a mission: Get in, get out, get home! Hurry, hurry. When we shop at the farmers' market, something magical happens. When you see someone you know, you stop, linger, catch up, show each other what you've bought, and talk about recipes. It's not uncommon to find yourself part of a three- or four-way conversation, sometimes with complete strangers and often with the farmer selling the salad greens, lamb chops, or farmstead cheese. This is the same sense of community that was embodied by county fairs and market days in small towns. It's a wonderful way to spend some time, link up with a friend or make a new one, and invest in your community.

When we begin slowly but surely to rearrange our lives in a manner that allows us to cook and share this way, we find we worry less about the overprocessed foods and hidden health hazards in our conventional food system. We find that we can rest easy, knowing that our children are eating, sharing, and loving nutritious, wholesome food every day. What on planet Earth can be better than that?

Chapter 1

THE SUSTAINABLE PANTRY

Home cooks have lost the habit of cooking ahead, of setting aside a block of time—perhaps 2 or 3 hours on a weekend afternoon—to cook for the coming week. Not only can this be enjoyable and relaxing, it also sets you up for nutritious and satisfying meals all week long.

There are two other benefits to this kind of cooking as well, both of which I particularly champion. First and foremost, it is a good way to bring the family into the kitchen to work together. As a father of five, I know how rewarding this can be. Second, it saves money and valuable resources, something that appeals to every household in these uncertain times. Supermarket checkout tallies rise when you buy a lot of packaged, canned, frozen, and processed foods; they decline as you buy food in the most natural condition offered in the market. (Yet another benefit: You'll have less packaging to dispose of.)

I am not suggesting you prepare full-blown meals on Sunday afternoon and freeze them. Instead, I urge you to prepare foods that can serve as your own convenience food, the building blocks of quick, nutritious meals. Cook legumes, grains, and vegetables in ways that make them easy to use throughout the week. Make large quantities of stock every now and then, and freeze it for later use in soups, braises, and sauces. Bake a few loaves of bread, and freeze them for sandwiches, French toast, and snacks. If the season is right, put up tomatoes or make jam for future consumption.

Believe me, when this kind of cooking becomes part of the family routine, everyone wins. Meals will be more healthful as you rely more on whole grains, roasted fresh vegetables, and legumes and less on convenience and processed foods. You and your kids will come to take pleasure in the time in the kitchen, chopping, measuring, and stirring—all easy and basic cooking chores that nonetheless teach useful life skills. I am not such an idealist that I think every child and every adult will love this idea, but try it before you dismiss it. You may be surprised. We are gung ho about attending every soccer and softball game our kids participate in, and why not? It's fun! I urge you to give equal time to cooking together to feed the family well and do a small part to save the planet at the same time.

As you read through the recipes in this chapter, you will note that many are for grains, which are crucial to a healthful diet. I thank the heavens that we've left the foolhardy era of no-carb, low-carb diets behind. Countless studies indicate that complex carbohydrates are essential and that we are genetically hardwired to eat them. The trick is choosing the right carbohydrates. Very few "good carbs" are readily available in the supermarket, where you are more likely to find the highly processed carbohydrates that have added inches to our waistlines over the years. Think high-fructose corn syrup (found in hundreds of products), white bread, white pasta, white rice, and breakfast cereal.

Ancient grains like farro were agricultural discoveries that allowed humans to convert from wandering bands of animal-seeking nomads to civilized cultures that could build settlements and eventually towns and states. Known as staples, grains like farro, spelt, rice, wheat, and beans (which I group with grains because of their culinary status, healthful properties, and similar cooking requirements) allowed civilizations to feed growing populations. Ancient grain staples were the very first foods to provide growing cultures with "food security." They can do the same for our families.

You will also see a few recipes for hash here. While neither the pork nor beef hash is a staple, the recipes are so versatile and delicious I had to include them. These are examples of how I suggest you use leftovers to create totally new dishes that taste as good as or better than the originals. The hash recipes are great with eggs, pasta, or grains or on their own for a quick and easy meal.

As you wander through your farmers' market, supermarket, natural foods store, or any other food market, think about what you could prepare easily (roasted vegetables, simply cooked barley) to use later in the week. What do your kids like? What would you like them to develop a taste for? What are your favorites? As you prepare meals, think about how you could use the leftovers. Take the time to bake bread and let the kids witness the miracle of active dry yeast, or make some jam to keep in the refrigerator for a few weeks to eat with the bread. Yes, it takes some planning, but in the long run, your family will be better fed, healthy, and happy.

The Sustainable Pantry

Roasted Carrots

Roasted Parsnips

Dried Heirloom Beans

Cooked Farro or Black Barley

Black-Eyed Peas

Old-Fashioned Honey-Wheat Bread

Pork Hash

Beef Hash

Savory Vegetable Stock

Put-Up Tomatoes

Savory Blackberry Jam

ROASTED CARROTS

You can fill whole baking sheets with carrots or parsnips—or beets, for that matter—for roasting. They are wonderful eaten as soon as they are roasted, with butter or a little oil, but because they taste good at any temperature, they are great to have on hand for all sorts of uses. Add these roasted vegetables to farro or hash, eat as a snack—kids like them—or use them for crudités platters.

Serves 4 to 6

2 TABLESPOONS GRAPESEED OIL

6–8 CARROTS, WASHED AND PEELED

KOSHER SALT AND FRESHLY GROUND BLACK PEPPER

Preheat the oven to 375°F.

Lightly oil the carrots. Season with salt and pepper.

Spread the carrots on a baking sheet. Roast for about 25 minutes, turning once, until they are lightly browned and tender and you can easily insert a toothpick or fork.

ROASTED PARSNIPS

Serves 4 to 6

2 TABLESPOONS UNSALTED BUTTER, AT ROOM TEMPERATURE

4 LARGE PARSNIPS, PEELED AND CUT IN HALF LENGTHWISE
   (CUT OUT ANY CORES THAT SEEM TOUGH OR WOODY)

KOSHER SALT AND FRESHLY GROUND BLACK PEPPER

Preheat the oven to 375°F.

Lightly spread the butter on the cut side of each parsnip half. Arrange cut side down on a baking sheet. Roast for about 35 minutes, or until they are browned and softened and you can easily insert a toothpick or fork. For moister parsnips, cover lightly with foil.

DRIED HEIRLOOM BEANS

When you can't get fresh beans, dried beans are a good option. Cooked properly, these legumes taste wonderful added to any number of dishes, such as soups, spreads, and sides. Don't be tempted to open a can of beans when it's so easy to cook dried beans and have them on hand when you need them. Take your time when you cook the beans; turning up the heat won't make anything go faster—it will just cause the beans to break apart.

Serves 6

2 CUPS DRIED BEANS, SUCH AS CRANBERRY, INDIAN WOMAN,
    APPALOOSA, OR LIMA BEANS

5–6 FRESH THYME SPRIGS

2 GARLIC CLOVES, PEELED OR UNPEELED

½ FRESH BAY LEAF

PINCH OF BAKING SODA

SEA SALT

1–2 TABLESPOONS UNSALTED BUTTER

1–2 TEASPOONS FRESH THYME LEAVES

Put the beans in a bowl and cover generously with cool water. Let the beans soak for at least 8 hours and up to 24 hours. Change the water several times during the soaking process, if you can.

Transfer the beans to a large saucepan and cover generously with water. Add the thyme, garlic, bay leaf, and baking soda. The baking soda helps soften the beans' skin. (Do not add salt to the water; salt toughens the beans.)

Bring the water to a simmer over medium heat. Reduce the heat to low and simmer very gently, partially covered, for about 2 hours, or until the beans are nice and tender.

Sprinkle enough salt into the water until the water tastes as salty as seawater. Remove the saucepan from the heat. Let it stand for 15 to 20 minutes, or until the beans are perfectly salted. At this point the beans can be drained, cooled, and refrigerated for up to 5 days or used in recipes that call for cooked dried heirloom beans.

To serve right away, drain the beans and serve hot, tossed with the butter and thyme.

COOKED FARRO
or BLACK BARLEY

This recipe is a very basic one for cooking two grains you may be unfamiliar with. The process is similar to cooking rice, but the grains benefit from being soaked for several hours first.

Makes about 5 cups

2 CUPS RAW FARRO OR BLACK BARLEY

Cover the farro or barley with boiling water in a large stockpot. Cover and set aside to soak for 3 to 4 hours.

Drain and rinse the grain. Return to the pot.

Cover the grain with 8 cups of cold water. Bring to a boil over high heat. Reduce the heat and simmer gently for 15 to 20 minutes, or until the grain is tender but not splitting open. Drain and use as directed. The cooked grain will keep in a covered container for up to 1 month in the refrigerator.

BLACK BARLEY

BLACK BARLEY IS ONE OF MY FAVORITE WHOLE GRAINS BECAUSE OF ITS BEAUTY WHEN RAW AS WELL AS COOKED AND ALSO BECAUSE OF ITS MEATY, FILLING, AND COMFORTING FLAVOR AND TEXTURE. THE GREAT NEWS ABOUT THIS AND ANY HEALTHFUL WHOLE GRAIN IS THAT IT NEEDS ONLY TO BE SIMMERED UNTIL TENDER, AND THEN YOU CAN USE IT ANY WAY YOU WANT: ADD IT TO A SOUP OR STEW OR COOK IT PILAF-STYLE, AS IN THE RECIPE ON PAGE 196. IT'S SO EASY, SO GOOD FOR YOU, AND SO, SO GOOD.

FORTUNATELY, MORE PEOPLE ARE BEGINNING TO DISCOVER HOW DELICIOUS THESE HEALTHFUL WHOLE GRAINS ARE. WHOLE GRAINS USED TO SUFFER FROM THE STIGMA THAT "IF IT'S GOOD FOR YOU, IT CAN'T TASTE GOOD," WHICH ALSO ASSUMED THEIR HIGH CONCENTRATION OF SOLUBLE FIBER WOULD HAVE UNWANTED SIDE EFFECTS. THE FACT IS THAT YOUR BODY REACTS FAR MORE FAVORABLY TO A GRAIN SUCH AS BLACK BARLEY THAN TO ANY OF THE UBIQUITOUS FIBER SUPPLEMENTS ON THE MARKET.

BLACK BARLEY AND OTHER UNFAMILIAR GRAINS ARE AVAILABLE ONLINE AND ALSO FROM MANY NATURAL FOOD STORES. YOU MAY HAVE TO BUY THEM IN RELATIVELY LARGE SACKS, BUT HONESTLY, I WOULD BE DELIGHTED TO SEE YOU EMPTY YOUR CUPBOARDS OF CONVERTED AND INSTANT RICE AND REPLACE THESE PRODUCTS WITH SEVERAL POUNDS OF BLACK BARLEY.

BLACK-EYED PEAS

Black-eyed peas are a famous American legume with a long culinary history stemming from the regions of the South where African, Caribbean, French, Creole, and Cajun influences have paired them with smoked meats, onions, and chiles—foods that beans love to hang around with. The only northern bean dish that rivals black-eyed peas is Boston baked beans, which are loaded with sweet molasses and sugar. I prefer black-eyed peas because I was raised by farmers from the southern Midwest—and I don't believe in dessert as a side dish.

You don't have to soak black-eyed peas as long as I do, but it won't hurt them. I find it easier to soak them overnight so that they are ready for me the next morning. I like to sit down to a whole bowl of these legumes, as the taste and texture of perfectly cooked black-eyed peas are just wonderful.

Serves 6

2 POUNDS DRIED BLACK-EYED PEAS

10 OUNCES HOG JOWL, LEFT IN 1 CHUNK

1 SMOKED HAM HOCK

1 LARGE ONION, QUARTERED

1 SERRANO OR JALAPEÑO CHILE PEPPER, HALVED AND SEEDED
    (WEAR PLASTIC GLOVES WHEN HANDLING)

2 TEASPOONS MOLASSES

SEA SALT AND FRESHLY GROUND BLACK PEPPER

Soak the peas in cool water to cover in a large bowl for at least 6 hours and up to 12 hours.

Cover the hog jowl and ham hock with water by 2" to 3" in a stockpot. Bring to a boil over high heat. Reduce the heat to medium-low and simmer for about $1\frac{1}{2}$ hours. During cooking, skim the foam that rises to the surface several times.

Drain the peas. Add them to the pot with the jowl and hock. Add the onion, chile pepper, and molasses. Do not add salt at this time. If there is not sufficient stock to cover the peas, add water until there is. Cover tightly and simmer gently over low heat for about 2 hours, or until the peas are tender and the liquid has been absorbed. Season to taste with salt and black pepper and serve.

OLD-FASHIONED HONEY-WHEAT BREAD

Homemade bread is awesome. If you haven't baked any in a while (or ever), don't wait much longer. There are any number of whole grain options available when you are choosing bread flour, and they are the best choices for great flavor and better health. For this recipe, you can use just about any whole grain flour, such as those milled from white winter wheat, hard red winter wheat (my favorite), or spring red wheat, which is a little softer than the other two. The final texture of the bread will vary a little depending on which you select, but the flours demonstrate their true differences when it comes to the flavor of the loaf. All are delicious.

I find it helps to add a little all-purpose flour to the dough to lighten the loaves, and a touch of honey sweetens them just a bit. This is the bread to bake on a weekend afternoon when you have time to knead the dough and let it rise 3 times. The result is a fine-grained, all-around bread perfect for toast or sandwiches. Although it's a good idea to let the loaves cool completely first so that the crumb forms perfectly, I like to sample bread warm from the oven— just because who can resist?

By the way, www.homegrownharvest.com is a great Web site for whole grain flours and other whole grain products.

Makes 2 loaves

2½ TEASPOONS ACTIVE DRY YEAST (ONE ¼-OUNCE PACKAGE)

2¾ CUPS LUKEWARM WATER

4 CUPS WHOLE WHEAT FLOUR

2 CUPS UNBLEACHED OR ALL-PURPOSE FLOUR

2 TEASPOONS SALT

3 TABLESPOONS LOCAL HONEY

2 TABLESPOONS GRAPESEED OIL

Stir the yeast into ½ cup of the water in a small bowl. Set aside to dissolve, bubble, and foam.

Stir together the whole wheat flour, all-purpose flour, and salt in a large bowl. Make a well in the center of the flour.

Meanwhile, dissolve the honey in the remaining 2¼ cups of water. Stir the oil into the water. Pour the water and dissolved yeast into the well you made in the flour. Stir with a wooden spoon or your hands until a soft dough forms that pulls away from the sides of the bowl. Add a little more water or flour, if necessary, to make a smooth, soft dough.

Turn out the dough onto a lightly floured surface. Knead for at least 10 minutes, or until the dough is smooth and dry.

Put the dough in a large, dry bowl. Cover with a clean kitchen towel. Set aside in a warm place for $1\frac{1}{2}$ to 2 hours, or until the dough has doubled in bulk and when you press into the dough with your finger, the indentation remains.

Turn out onto a lightly floured surface. Knead, pushing against the dough to release the built-up gases. Gather into a ball. Let the dough rise again in the same bowl for 45 to 60 minutes, or until doubled.

Turn out onto a lightly floured surface. Knead gently again. Divide the dough in half and form each half into a loaf shape. Put each half into an oiled 8" or 9" × $3\frac{1}{2}$" loaf pan. Cover with the kitchen towel and let rise for 40 to 45 minutes, or until the loaves fill the pans and rise to the top.

Preheat the oven to 425°F.

Bake the loaves for 10 minutes. Reduce the heat to 325°F and bake for 50 to 55 minutes longer, or until the loaves are risen and golden brown. When the bread slides out of the pan, the bottom of the loaf should sound hollow when tapped.

Let the loaves cool completely on racks.

PORK HASH

I developed this and the following recipe for beef hash to use leftover Smothered Pork Chops or leftover Beef Short Rib Pot Roast, but you could make them with other leftover pork or beef. While it's a little tricky to find substitutes for the leftover gravies, you can use chicken or beef stock in a pinch. Hash is great with eggs, added to casseroles, or eaten with some good bread and a salad for an easy, light meal. Enjoy!

Makes about 4½ cups

3 CUPS SHREDDED COOKED PORK FROM LEFTOVER SMOTHERED
   PORK CHOPS (PAGE 160) OR OTHER LEFTOVER PORK

1 CUP GRAVY FROM LEFTOVER SMOTHERED PORK CHOPS
   OR CHICKEN STOCK

½ CUP CUBED ROASTED CARROTS (PAGE 4)

½ CUP DICED ROASTED PARSNIPS (PAGE 4)

¾–1 CUP HEIRLOOM MASHED POTATOES (PAGE 211)

3 TABLESPOONS CHOPPED FRESH HERBS, SUCH AS THYME
   OR PARSLEY

KOSHER SALT AND FRESHLY GROUND BLACK PEPPER

1 CUP COARSE BREAD CRUMBS, SUCH AS PANKO

2 TABLESPOONS GRAPESEED OIL

Use your hands or a large wooden spoon to mix together the pork, gravy, carrots, parsnips, and mashed potatoes in a large bowl. Add the herbs. Taste, and season with salt and pepper. The hash is ready to use for Pork Hash and Scrambled Eggs (page 43). You could also freeze it at this point for up to a month.

To cook the hash, form the mixture into patties.

Spread the bread crumbs in a shallow dish. Press the patties into the crumbs to coat lightly on both sides.

Heat the oil in a large skillet over medium-high heat. When hot, cook the hash patties for 3 to 4 minutes on each side, or until lightly browned and heated through. The patties will sag a little. Serve immediately.

BEEF HASH

This is a loose-style hash and can be used in a variety of dishes, such as the Beef Hash and Poached Eggs on page 44. Or, after it's been sautéed, toss it with your favorite pasta. You can also simmer it in a rich brown stock to make soup. Just add cooked grains (page 10) to make a hearty meal.

Makes about 4½ cups

3 CUPS SHREDDED LEFTOVER BEEF FROM BEEF SHORT-RIB POT ROAST (PAGE 171)

1 CUP LEFTOVER GRAVY FROM BEEF SHORT-RIB POT ROAST

½ CUP CUBED ROASTED CARROTS (PAGE 4)

½ CUP CUBED ROASTED PARSNIPS (PAGE 4)

¾–1 CUP ROASTED POTATOES

KOSHER SALT AND FRESHLY GROUND BLACK PEPPER

2 TABLESPOONS GRAPESEED OIL

Preheat the oven to 350°F.

In a large bowl, mix together the beef, gravy, carrots, parsnips, and potatoes. Taste, and season with salt and pepper.

Heat the oil in a large skillet over medium-high heat. When hot, cook the hash for 3 to 4 minutes, stirring until lightly browned and heated through. Serve immediately.

SAVORY VEGETABLE STOCK

It's not uncommon to find ourselves in a "state of need" when it comes to stock, especially when we set about making soups, stews, and grain porridges. Vegetable stocks are very simple to make, as they use easy-to-obtain vegetables and do not require long cooking. Nothing could be more straightforward to make than one of these brews: You literally just add water and let the veggies simmer for an hour or so. Plus, these stocks are a safe bet if you have any worries about your guests' allergies or vegetarian tendencies.

Most recipes that call for stock have either a savory or sweet profile. For savory soups, such as the Garden Gazpacho on page 74, you need a savory vegetable stock, such as this one. For a sweeter dish, such as the Nantucket Scallop Porridge with Apples and Chestnuts on page 81, you want a sweeter stock, made with root vegetables. For either of these stocks—or any other vegetable stock, for that matter—roasting the vegetables first will yield a richer, more flavorful broth. If you do this, cut the simmering time for the stock in half.

How do you know whether you want savory or sweet? The ingredients are great clues. If a recipe calls for hard squash, pumpkin, or any type of fruit, sweet is the way to go. If the dish is tangy, lemony, or focused on earthy flavors—think about mushrooms or hot peppers—savory is key. Both of these basic stocks are easy to make and easy to store.

Makes about 4 quarts

I FENNEL BULB, TRIMMED AND QUARTERED

3 LARGE LEEKS, TRIMMED AND COARSELY CHOPPED

3 LARGE ONIONS, PEELED AND QUARTERED

I RUTABAGA, PEELED AND COARSELY CHOPPED

I POUND MUSHROOM STEMS OR WHOLE MUSHROOMS

Combine the vegetables in a large stockpot. Add enough water to cover by an inch.

Bring to a boil over high heat. Immediately reduce the heat. Simmer gently for about 1½ hours, or until the stock is nicely flavored.

Strain the stock. Let it cool to room temperature. When cool, transfer to lidded containers and refrigerate for up to 1 week. (Save and refrigerate any vegetables that do not feel grossly overcooked. These veggies are a great addition to any hash recipe, such as on pages 43 and 44.)

PUT-UP TOMATOES

There was a time when canning tomatoes was as common as making eggs for breakfast. When we were a more agrarian society, no one thought of buying cans of tomatoes during winter months. Instead, they grabbed a jar or two from the cellar and rejoiced in the flavor of home-grown tomatoes that had been preserved at the peak of their ripeness. Nowadays, it may seem there is no reason to go to the trouble of canning—except that they taste so good and make January meals happy events bathed in the memory of last summer. You'll also know exactly where the tomatoes came from, and, without a doubt, the tomatoes you grow yourself or find at a local farmers' market will be far tastier than store-bought canned tomatoes.

Canning is a seasonal task, best accomplished when you have access to at least a half bushel of ripe summer tomatoes. For us, living in Connecticut, this is generally around Labor Day. Depending on where you live, it might be a little earlier or later. We have found that a half bushel yields about 8 quarts. While tomatoes themselves are acidic, pouring a little lemon juice into each jar ups the acid and ensures the safety of the tomatoes.

Although you don't need a lot of special equipment, you will need at least 8 quart jars (I recommend having a few extra in case the tomatoes fill more than 8 jars or in the event one breaks) with new lids and rings. You also will need a large pot, such as a canning pot or deep stockpot with about a 21-quart capacity. A jar lifter is handy, but both my coauthor, Mary, and I have been known to get by with good tongs and thick pot holders. If you have a canner jar rack that fits in the pot, so much the better.

Set aside a few hours to can the tomatoes, and expect a damp, humid kitchen.

Makes 8 quart jars

½ BUSHEL TOMATOES

1 CUP FRESH LEMON JUICE (4–5 LEMONS)

8–12 FRESH BASIL LEAVES (OPTIONAL)

Fill a large, deep pot about halfway with water. Cover and set it on a back burner over high heat to come to a boil. When it boils, turn off the heat, but leave the lid on to keep the water as hot as possible.

Fill a large saucepan about halfway with water. Bring to a simmer over medium-high heat. Fill a large bowl or the sink with cold water.

Immerse 2 or 3 tomatoes in the simmering water for 50 to 60 seconds. Lift them from the water with a slotted spoon and plunge into the cold water. When cool, slip off and discard the skins. Transfer the peeled tomatoes to a bowl. Repeat until all the tomatoes are peeled. You will have to change the water several times to keep it cold. You may also want to replenish the saucepan of simmering water.

(continued)

With a sharp paring knife, remove and discard the core from the tomatoes and cut each into halves or quarters, depending on their size.

Put the tomatoes into a sterilized quart canning jar (see "How to Sterilize the Jars and Lids" on page 27). Push as many tomato pieces as you can into the jar to fill it to within $\frac{1}{4}$" of the rim. Work around the edges of the jar with the handle of a long-handled, clean wooden spoon to expel any air bubbles. After you do this, you may be able to fit another quarter or half tomato into the jar.

Add 2 tablespoons of the lemon juice to the jar. You can also add a leaf or two of basil, if desired. Wipe the rim of each jar with a clean, dry kitchen towel to free it of stray seeds or liquid. Set a sterilized lid on the jar. Secure it with a screw-on ring. Repeat until you have filled as many jars as you can with tomatoes.

Let the water in the large pot return to a boil over high heat. Submerge the jars in the water using a jar lifter or sturdy tongs. If the water does not cover the jars, add more hot water (from a boiling kettle is best) until they are completely covered with water.

Let the jars boil in the water for 45 to 50 minutes. Remove the jars from the water bath with the jar lifter or tongs, and set them on a dry kitchen towel to cool. Leave ample room for air to circulate between the jars, and do not let them touch each other as they cool.

Leave the jars undisturbed until completely cool, usually 8 hours or overnight. When they are cool, check that the lids are concave. Do this by pushing on the lids with your finger. There should be no movement or give. (If any are not concave, remove the lid and transfer the tomatoes to a refrigerator container, and use as soon as you can.) Remove the rings, which can be used again, and store the lidded jars in a cool, dry place. They will keep for 1 year, at least.

SAFETY ISSUES WHEN CANNING TOMATOES

Canning acidic ingredients such as tomatoes is easy and safe. It requires only sterilized canning jars and a deep pot of water (no pressure cooking involved). It's easy to tell right from the beginning if the process worked: Once the jars cool, the lids will be obviously concave. In fact, during cooling you might hear a slight "sucking" sound. That's the sound of the vacuum inside the jar fixing the lid so that the seal is as tight as can be. Another way to tell if the vacuum has formed is to tap the lids with a spoon before the jars cool and then tap them afterward. The sound of a properly sealed lid will be deep and resonant, while the sound of a lid that has not yet formed the vacuum is tinny.

When you open the jar, it will release with a reassuring pop, which indicates the tomatoes are as fresh as when you pushed them into the jar. It might reassure you to know that if the seal breaks and the tomatoes spoil, you will know it as soon as you remove the lid: The tomatoes will foam and sputter in ways that are not normal.

SAVORY BLACKBERRY JAM

I recommend you spoon this alongside meat and poultry, although it's also good spread on toast and biscuits. Jams are simple to make, which is good news because when the berries are ripe, they come at us fast and furious, and it's gratifying to be able to make jam. The result is fantastic, and there is nothing quite like the sense of pride you get when you open a jar of homemade jam. While this jam is not processed in a water bath for longtime storage, it does keep in the refrigerator for several months. I doubt it will be around that long!

Makes 2 pints

3 PINTS BLACKBERRIES

1 JALAPEÑO CHILE PEPPER, SEEDED AND THINLY SLICED (WEAR PLASTIC GLOVES WHEN HANDLING)

1 SMALL RED ONION, DICED

1 CINNAMON STICK

¼ CUP RAW SUGAR

2 TABLESPOONS HONEY

ZEST AND JUICE OF 1 LEMON

Rinse the berries very well and let them drain. Three pints will provide 6 cups of berries.

Puree 4 cups of the blackberries in a blender until smooth. Pass the puree through a fine-mesh sieve into a saucepan, using the back of a wooden spoon to force everything but the seeds through the sieve.

Add the pepper, onion, cinnamon stick, sugar, honey, lemon zest, and lemon juice. Bring to a simmer over medium-low heat. Simmer uncovered for 25 to 30 minutes, or until the mixture reaches a jamlike consistency and coats the back of the spoon.

Add the rest of the berries and simmer for 4 to 6 minutes. Remove and discard the cinnamon stick.

Transfer the jam to 2 clean pint jars. Fill both to about $\frac{1}{4}$" below the screw threads. Tighten the lid on the jar and invert the jar onto its lid. Let it cool to room temperature.

Store the jam in the refrigerator for up to 3 months.

HOW TO STERILIZE THE JARS AND LIDS

Some dishwashers have a "sterilize" cycle, which is a good way to make sure your jars are as clean as can be. Otherwise, start with clean jars that you have washed in hot, soapy water and then rinsed well. Submerge them in the canning pot filled with boiling water. Let the water boil around them for about 5 minutes, and leave them in the hot water with the heat switched off until you are ready to fill them. Clearly, this should not be done too long before canning.

Canning lids are flat with a rubber ring around the inside. Sterilize them, too, in a pan of boiling water. Lift them out with tongs or a lid-lifting tool (which is magnetized to grip the lids). You can reuse the screw-on rings from year to year, but the screw-on lids are good for only onetime use. The lids will rust if you leave them on the jars during storage.

Chapter 2

BREAKFAST

For so many of us, breakfast is the great American meal. For generations, it set us up for a long day's work in the fields, factories, and mines, and for a lot of us, this has not changed. We still look to breakfast to sustain us before we set off for the day. What has changed is the menu.

We have gone from eating eggs and small portions of meat and fruits and whole grain breads hardy enough to wrap in a napkin and slip in a jacket pocket to sugar-coated cereals and jammy things that we stick in a toaster. Breakfast is a good opportunity to reverse this trend. Armed with a nutritious breakfast, we all have a good chance of making it to lunchtime without distracting hunger pangs. The calories from complex carbohydrates and protein transform to glucose and nutrients slowly, the way it should be, sustaining the feeling of satiety throughout the morning.

You may not have time to make these recipes every day, and on the days you cannot, serve whole grain breads and cereals, oatmeal made from steel-cut rolled oats, and scrambled eggs now and then. When you do have time, make my frittatas, omelets, home fries, and homemade hash for super breakfasts. Your family will thank you!

PULLET EGGS WITH CURED PORK BELLY

BREAKFAST FRITTATA

FORAGED FRITTATA

LOBSTER BREAKFAST

FISHERMAN'S BREAKFAST

SPICY SAUSAGE OMELET WITH FRESH VEGETABLES

BREAKFAST SAUSAGE

PORK HASH AND SCRAMBLED EGGS

BEEF HASH AND POACHED EGGS

HEIRLOOM POTATO HOME FRIES

WHOLE GRAIN FRUIT AND VEGETABLE BREAD

FRENCH TOAST WITH BROWN SUGAR BANANAS

BREAKFAST PORRIDGE

PULLET EGGS
with CURED PORK BELLY

This recipe is about the eggs but also about the pork belly. I "cure" the meat with herbs and sugar and salt and then roast it, at which point it's ready to slice and cook just like bacon. It tastes a little like bacon but is somewhat stronger. I like it better.

Serves 4 to 6

I CUP KOSHER SALT

I CUP SUGAR

I TEASPOON FRESHLY GROUND BLACK PEPPER

I TEASPOON GROUND CORIANDER SEEDS

$\frac{1}{4}$ TEASPOON GROUND ANISE

2 WHOLE CLOVES

2 BAY LEAVES, BROKEN IN PIECES

I POUND PORK BELLY

I DOZEN ORGANIC PULLET EGGS OR ANY HIGH-QUALITY ORGANIC
   HEN EGGS

Stir together the salt and sugar in a mixing bowl. Spread half of this mixture in the bottom of a glass or ceramic dish large enough to hold the pork belly.

Mix together the pepper, coriander seeds, anise, cloves, and bay leaves in another small bowl. Sprinkle the pork belly with the spice mixture. Rub it into all sides. Put the pork in the dish on top of the salt-and-sugar mixture. Spread the remaining sugar and salt over the meat. Cover and refrigerate for at least 24 hours and up to 36 hours.

Preheat the oven to 300°F.

Lift the pork belly from the dish and rinse the meat with cool running water to remove the spices. Pat dry with paper towels then place in a roasting pan. Roast, fat side up, for about $1\frac{1}{2}$ hours, or until some of the fat renders and begins to brown. Remove the pork belly from the oven. Set aside to cool completely. When cool, wrap the pork belly in plastic wrap or put in a clean dish. Refrigerate for at least 4 hours and up to 24 hours, until chilled.

Slice the pork belly across the grain into strips that resemble thick bacon. Each slice should be about $\frac{1}{4}$" thick.

In a large skillet over medium heat, fry the slices of pork belly for 6 to 8 minutes, or until crisp and browned. Spoon off the fat as it renders so that the pork slices are not swimming in fat. Drain the slices on paper towels.

Bring a deep skillet filled with water to a rapid simmer over medium heat. Crack one of the eggs onto a saucer or similar small dish. Slide the egg into the water and poach for 2 to 3 minutes, or until the white sets. Repeat with the remaining eggs. With a slotted spoon, lift the poached eggs from the poaching water and serve on a plate with the fried pork belly.

BREAKFAST FRITTATA

A frittata is not just an open-faced omelet, and this recipe proves it. This may be a slightly unorthodox way of making a frittata—starting it in the top of a double boiler, which makes the eggs especially moist and creamy, and then finishing it in a skillet—but the results are well worth it. The eggs pick up the flavors of the vegetables and other ingredients as they cook.

Serves 4 to 6

3 TABLESPOONS EXTRA-VIRGIN OLIVE OIL

12 LARGE EGGS

½ CUP COARSELY CHOPPED, ROASTED, AND COLLAPSED
    EGGPLANT FLESH (SEE NOTE)

½ CUP COARSELY CHOPPED LEFTOVER WILTED SPINACH OR
    OTHER GREENS

1 ROASTED RED BELL PEPPER, PEELED, SEEDED, AND SLICED
    INTO ¼"–½"-WIDE STRIPS

4 ROASTED GARLIC CLOVES, SMASHED (SEE NOTE)

2 TABLESPOONS FRESH THYME

2 TABLESPOONS UNSALTED BUTTER, AT ROOM TEMPERATURE

¾ CUP COARSELY CRUMBLED SOFT GOAT CHEESE

2 TABLESPOONS GRAPESEED OIL

¼ CUP FRESH BREAD CRUMBS, TOSSED WITH 1 TABLESPOON
    OLIVE OIL

Preheat the oven to 400°F.

Prepare a double boiler by bringing the water in the base to a simmer over medium heat. (If you do not have a double boiler, use a saucepan set over a slightly larger pan holding a little water.) Heat the olive oil in the top of the double boiler over the simmering water until hot.

Note: I LIKE TO ROAST HALVED OR QUARTERED EGGPLANT IN A 375°F OVEN FOR 35 TO 40 MINUTES (DEPENDING ON THE SIZE OF THE EGGPLANT), OR UNTIL IT SOFTENS AND FEELS VERY TENDER WHEN PIERCED WITH A KNIFE. YOU CAN ALSO USE GRILLED EGGPLANT FOR THIS RECIPE. HALVE OR QUARTER THE EGGPLANT, SPRINKLE THE CUT SIDES WITH OLIVE OIL AND SALT, AND ROAST, CUT SIDES DOWN. LET THE ROASTED EGGPLANT COOL FOR ABOUT 10 MINUTES, DURING WHICH TIME THE FLESH WILL COLLAPSE. YOU CAN USE LEFTOVER COOKED EGGPLANT FOR THIS AS LONG AS IT'S NOT TOO HEAVILY SEASONED.

Add the eggs and cook for about 5 minutes, stirring constantly with a heatproof spatula or wooden spoon, until the eggs begin to thicken and scramble. Add the eggplant, greens, pepper, garlic, and thyme. Continue stirring until the eggs are the consistency of a very soft scramble. Stir in the butter until fully incorporated. Add ½ cup of the goat cheese, barely stirring it into the eggs and being careful to leave the crumbles intact.

Meanwhile, heat a cast-iron skillet over medium heat.

Rub the hot skillet with a clean kitchen towel that has been lightly dipped in the grapeseed oil. Immediately pour the egg mixture into the skillet. *Do not stir!* Use a spatula or wooden spoon to ensure the egg mixture is spread evenly. Top with the remaining ¼ cup of goat cheese crumbles and the bread crumbs.

Transfer the skillet to the oven. Cook for 5 to 7 minutes, or until the eggs are more set and the bread crumbs are browned.

Note: TO ROAST GARLIC, WRAP THE CLOVES IN A SMALL PIECE OF ALUMINUM FOIL, SPRINKLE WITH A LITTLE OLIVE OIL, AND ROAST IN A 350°F OVEN FOR ABOUT 30 MINUTES. REMOVE THE CLOVES FROM THE FOIL AND SQUEEZE THE ROASTED PULP FROM THE CLOVES. USING THE SIDE OF A LARGE KNIFE, SMASH THE PULP. WHILE THIS RECIPE CALLS FOR ONLY 4 CLOVES OF ROASTED GARLIC, YOU MAY FIND IT MORE EFFICIENT TO ROAST AN ENTIRE HEAD. STORE THE ROASTED GARLIC IN THE REFRIGERATOR AND ADD THE CLOVES TO OTHER FRITTATAS AND EGG DISHES, SPREADS, AND CRUSTY BREAD DRIZZLED WITH GOOD OLIVE OIL. TO ROAST A HEAD OF GARLIC, SLICE A THIN LAYER FROM THE TOP OF THE HEAD TO EXPOSE THE INDIVIDUAL CLOVES. WRAP THE HEAD IN FOIL SPRINKLED WITH OLIVE OIL AND ROAST AS ABOVE, BUT FOR 30 TO 35 MINUTES.

GOOD EGGS

THERE WAS A TIME WHEN EGGS WERE NOT PACKAGED IN PLASTIC OR CARDBOARD CARTONS OR GRADED LARGE, EXTRA LARGE, AND JUMBO. INSTEAD, THEY WERE SOLD FROM CAREFULLY PACKED BASKETS, OFTEN STILL WARM FROM THE HEN. FOLKS RECOGNIZED THAT DIFFERENT EGGS WERE GOOD FOR DIFFERENT COOKING METHODS AND THAT PULLET EGGS WERE ESPECIALLY GOOD FOR POACHING—A TECHNIQUE THAT LETS THE EGG STAND ALONE WITHOUT ANY FLOURISHES OR FLAVORINGS. PULLET EGGS ARE THE FIRST EGGS LAID BY IMMATURE CHICKENS, SO THEY'RE SMALL IN SIZE YET RICH IN FLAVOR. IF YOU ARE FORTUNATE ENOUGH TO LIVE IN AN AREA WHERE YOU CAN BUY FRESH EGGS FROM A FARMER, TRY TO GET PULLET EGGS. YOU MAY HAVE TO KEEP GOING BACK TO THE FARM TO GET THE EGGS, BUT EVEN THAT CAN BE AN ADVENTURE, PARTICULARLY IF YOUR KIDS GET IN ON THE ACTION. IF YOU CAN'T FIND PULLET EGGS, SUBSTITUTE ANY ORGANIC EGGS. YOU CAN ALSO ORDER PULLET EGGS FROM HERITAGE FOODS USA.

FORAGED FRITTATA

The true delights of a dedicated forager are mushrooms and the wild greens that usually grow near them, such as ramps, lamb's-quarter, and sheep sorrel. For this frittata, I ask only that you forage at the farmers' market for a few varieties of wild mushrooms and for arugula and good slab bacon (although the cured pork belly on page 30 would do well here). Nothing beats the smokiness of the bacon mingling with the earthiness of the mushrooms and tang of the arugula when all are hugged by fresh eggs.

Serves 6

5 OUNCES SLAB BACON, CUT INTO ½" CUBES

3 TABLESPOONS GRAPESEED OIL

¼ TABLESPOON SLICED SHALLOTS

12 OUNCES FORAGED OR FARMERS' MARKET WILD MUSHROOMS,
    SUCH AS SHIITAKE, CHANTERELLE, AND OYSTER, CLEANED
    AND TRIMMED

5 OUNCES ARUGULA, CHOPPED

12 LARGE EGGS, WHISKED

5 OUNCES MILD CHEDDAR OR SHEEP'S MILK CHEESE, GRATED

2 TABLESPOONS UNSALTED BUTTER

SALT AND FRESHLY GROUND BLACK PEPPER

Preheat the oven to 450°F.

Cook the bacon in a skillet over medium-low heat for 5 to 7 minutes, or until cooked but not too crispy. Drain on paper towels.

Heat the oil in a large nonstick skillet over medium heat until hot. Add the shallots and cook for about 3 minutes, or until fully translucent. Add the mushrooms. Cover tightly and cook for about 5 minutes, or until the mushrooms wilt fully and exude their juices. Remove the lid. Cook for about 2 minutes, or until the pan is nearly dry.

Stir the arugula and bacon into the skillet with the mushrooms. Cook for about 1 minute, or until the arugula begins to wilt.

Add the eggs. Cook for about 2 minutes, stirring just until they begin to set but are still runny. Stir in half of the cheese and remove the skillet from the heat.

Heat an ovenproof, 8" cast-iron skillet over medium heat. When hot, melt the butter in it.

Season the eggs with salt and pepper to taste. Transfer the eggs to the hot cast-iron skillet. Sprinkle with the remaining cheese. Bake in the hot oven for 5 to 7 minutes, or until the cheese melts and is lightly browned and the eggs set. Serve directly from the pan.

LOBSTER BREAKFAST

Lobster for breakfast? Absolutely! It's more healthful than a lot of things we eat for breakfast—pain au chocolat, anyone?—and it turns the meal into something very special.

Serves 4

4 (1–1½ POUND) LIVE LOBSTERS (SEE NOTE)

2–3 TABLESPOONS UNSALTED BUTTER, MELTED

KOSHER SALT AND FRESHLY GROUND BLACK PEPPER

2 TABLESPOONS EXTRA-VIRGIN OLIVE OIL

8 LARGE EGGS

¼ CUP ROASTED EGGPLANT FLESH (SEE NOTE ON PAGE 32)

¼ CUP LEFTOVER WILTED SPINACH OR OTHER GREENS

1 ROASTED RED BELL PEPPER, CUT IN ¼"–½"-WIDE STRIPS

2–3 ROASTED GARLIC CLOVES, SMASHED

1 TABLESPOON FRESH THYME

2 TABLESPOONS UNSALTED BUTTER, AT ROOM TEMPERATURE

2–3 TABLESPOONS FRESH BREAD CRUMBS

Preheat the broiler to high. Set the broiler rack 6" to 8" below the heat unit. Prepare a double boiler by bringing the water in the base to a simmer over medium heat.

Split the lobsters in half and clean the cavities. Twist off the claws and crack gently. Arrange the lobster claws on a baking sheet. Broil for 2 to 3 minutes. Turn the claws over. Put the lobster halves, flesh side up, on the baking sheet. Brush the exposed flesh lightly with some of the melted butter. Season lightly with salt and black pepper. Return to the broiler and cook, basting twice with more of the melted butter, for 6 to 8 minutes, or until the lobster meat is nearly cooked through and opaque. Remove from the oven and keep warm. Do not turn off the broiler.

Heat the oil in the top of the double boiler. Add the eggs and cook, stirring constantly, until the eggs begin to thicken and scramble. Add the eggplant, greens, bell pepper, garlic, and thyme. Continue stirring until the eggs are the consistency of a very soft scramble. Stir in the softened butter.

Spoon the scrambled eggs into the cavities of the lobsters. Sprinkle the eggs with the bread crumbs and return the stuffed lobsters to the broiler. Cook until nicely browned and serve.

Note: TO KILL THE LOBSTERS, HOLD ONE ON A CUTTING BOARD BELLY-SIDE UP WITH THE HEAD POINTING AWAY FROM YOU. PLUNGE THE TIP OF A SHARP CHEF'S KNIFE STRAIGHT INTO THE BODY, AIMING FOR THE POINT ABOUT AN INCH FROM THE EYES TOWARD THE TAIL. WHEN THE KNIFE HAS GONE ALL THE WAY THROUGH THE LOBSTER AND HAS HIT THE CUTTING BOARD, BRING IT DOWN TO SPLIT THE LOBSTER IN HALF. THIS KILLS THE LOBSTER QUICKLY, WHILE SPLITTING THE BODY AND TAIL WITH ONE FIRM STROKE OF THE KNIFE. TURN THE LOBSTER AROUND SO THE HEAD IS FACING THE OTHER WAY AND FINISH CUTTING THE LOBSTER.

FISHERMAN'S BREAKFAST

When I was a kid, my dad and uncle Sherman often took my brothers and me fishing in Wisconsin, and if any one of us hooked a trout or walleyed pike, Uncle Sherman made breakfast for us. It might seem odd to eat fish with bacon and eggs, but to me—with my fond taste memories happily percolating—it sounds amazing. And it is.

Because everything is cooked in the same large skillet, the trick is to have the pan sitting partly off the heat source, a technique that allows you to cook some foods on the hot side of the pan while others keep warm on the cooler side. Of course, this is a common trick with campers, hunters, and fishermen who don't have the luxury of a fully stocked kitchen. But they do have the advantage of cooking out of doors, and, as anyone who has experienced it knows, food never tastes better than there!

Serves 4

½ CUP CORN FLOUR (I LIKE ANSON MILLS) OR CORNMEAL

4 TROUT FILLETS (4–6 OUNCES EACH)

SALT AND FRESHLY GROUND BLACK PEPPER

4 STRIPS THICK-CUT SLICED BACON

4 LARGE EGGS

Spread the corn flour on a shallow plate. Season each fish fillet with salt and pepper. Lightly dredge in the corn flour. Set aside.

Heat a large cast-iron skillet over medium heat. Cook the bacon until it begins to brown and turn crisp. Spoon off all but 2 tablespoons of the bacon fat and reserve it.

Scoot the cooked bacon to one side of the skillet. Adjust the skillet so that it's sitting only partially over the heat, with the bacon on the cool side, away from the heat.

Set the fillets on the hot side of the skillet. Cook the fillets for about 2½ minutes on each side, or until cooked through. Push to the side of the pan with the bacon and shingle the fillets next to the bacon.

If necessary, add some of the reserved bacon fat to the pan to lubricate it. Crack the eggs into the pan (or crack them one at a time into a small dish and slide them into the pan). Cook for 3 to 4 minutes, or until cooked sunny-side up. Serve with the trout and the bacon. And an ice-cold beer!

SPICY SAUSAGE OMELET
with FRESH VEGETABLES

Omelets make terrific breakfasts, although they are good for meals later in the day, too. If you can, use eggs that you have bought from a local farmer or at a farmers' market. The omelet will be markedly better. For a full-bodied meal, try this with the Creamy Cheese Grits on page 201 or Heirloom Potato Home Fries on page 46.

Serves 4

6 TABLESPOONS UNSALTED BUTTER

6 TABLESPOONS GRAPESEED OIL

2 UNCOOKED (RAW) CHORIZO SAUSAGES, REMOVED FROM CASINGS

1/2 ZUCCHINI, FINELY DICED

1/2 YELLOW SQUASH, FINELY DICED

1/2 RED ONION, FINELY DICED

1/2 RED BELL PEPPER, FINELY DICED

1 GARLIC CLOVE, MINCED

SALT AND FRESHLY GROUND BLACK PEPPER

12 LARGE ORGANIC EGGS

3/4 CUP + 2 TABLESPOONS HALF-AND-HALF OR WHOLE MILK

1/2 CUP SHREDDED FRESH MOZZARELLA CHEESE

3 TABLESPOONS FINELY CHOPPED FRESH BASIL

3 TABLESPOONS FINELY CHOPPED FLAT-LEAF PARSLEY

Heat 2 tablespoons of the butter and 2 tablespoons of the oil in a skillet over medium-high heat. When the butter melts, add the sausage and cook through, breaking the sausage into smaller pieces.

Add the zucchini, squash, onion, bell pepper, and garlic to the skillet. Continue to cook for 3 to 5 minutes, or until softened. Season to taste with salt and black pepper and stir well. Set aside.

Heat 1 tablespoon of the butter and 1 tablespoon of the oil in a 6" or 7" nonstick omelet pan over medium heat. Whisk together 3 eggs with 1 tablespoon of the half-and-half in a small bowl. Season with salt and black pepper. When the butter melts, pour the egg mixture into the pan. Stir the eggs with a wooden spoon until the eggs set. Add 2 to 3 tablespoons of the reserved vegetable filling and 2 tablespoons of the cheese to the center of the omelet.

Fold one side of the omelet over the filling. Tilt the pan toward the plate and slide the folded side onto the plate. As you do this, fold the other side over the filling, too. This maneuver takes practice, so don't be discouraged if you don't get it right away. Garnish the omelet with some of the basil and parsley and a little more filling and cheese.

Make 3 more omelets in the same fashion.

BREAKFAST SAUSAGE

One of the most universally beloved smells is that of sausage or bacon cooking in the morning. Not only is it incredibly enticing, it also means that someone cares enough to cook breakfast. Making your own sausage is easier than you might think, and it allows you to control what goes into it in terms of meat, fat, and salt—better yet, it has none of the nitrates and other chemicals that show up in commercial sausages. Ultimately, though, the best reason for making your own sausage is because it's just so damn good.

It's getting easier to find really good pork these days, particularly at farmers' markets. In addition to good pork, you will have to invest in a meat grinder, either an attachment for your standing mixer or a good table model. When you grind the meat and other ingredients, keep everything cold, including the grinding plates. This preserves the integrity of the ingredients.

Makes 8 to 10 patties: serves 4 to 6

2¼ POUNDS FRESH PORK SHOULDER, CUT INTO ¼" DICE

10 OUNCES PORK FATBACK (UNSALTED), CUT INTO ¼" DICE

1 TABLESPOON AGAVE NECTAR

2 TEASPOONS CHOPPED FRESH SAGE

1 TABLESPOON THINLY SLICED FRESH THYME

2 TEASPOONS THINLY SLICED FLAT-LEAF PARSLEY

½ TEASPOON FRESH GRATED NUTMEG OR MACE (OPTIONAL)

1 TABLESPOON SEA SALT

2 TEASPOONS FRESHLY GROUND BLACK PEPPER

2 SERRANO CHILE PEPPERS, FINELY MINCED

2 TABLESPOONS GRAPESEED OIL

Mix together all the ingredients except the oil in a large bowl. Cover and refrigerate for at least 2 hours and up to 12 hours. Chill the grinding plates for your meat grinder.

Fit a meat grinder with the large grinding plate. Push the meat through the grinder, and then return it to the bowl. Cover and refrigerate for 20 to 30 minutes.

Fit the meat grinder with the medium grinding plate. Push the meat through the grinder and put in a bowl. With dampened hands, form the ground meat into patties that are about 4" across. (You can make smaller or larger patties, if you prefer.)

Heat a heavy skillet over medium-low heat. When hot, add the oil and cook the patties for 6 to 7 minutes, or until nicely browned on one side. Turn over and cook for about 5 minutes longer, or until browned on the other side and cooked through. Check for doneness by piercing a sausage to see if it is fully cooked. If the center is pink, continue cooking until the meat is brown all the way through. Drain the sausages on paper towels and serve hot.

PORK HASH
and SCRAMBLED EGGS

Sausage and bacon are time-honored breakfast staples, but if you serve hash made from uncured leftover pork and therefore not packed with nitrates, making it a far healthier option, you are in for a real treat with your scrambled eggs. This hash is great made with leftovers from the Smothered Pork Chops on page 160, but you can use other leftover pork as well. I make the hash with parsnips and carrots, both appealingly sweet vegetables. And while you don't need the bread crumbs to finish the hash, they do give it a crispy crust that is a nice contrast to the soft eggs.

Serves 6

I CUP COARSE BREAD CRUMBS, SUCH AS PANKO

6 UNCOOKED PORK HASH PATTIES (PAGE 16)

2 TABLESPOONS GRAPESEED OIL

I TABLESPOON UNSALTED BUTTER

6 LARGE EGGS

I TABLESPOON SLICED FRESH CHIVES

KOSHER SALT AND FRESHLY GROUND BLACK PEPPER

Preheat the oven to 250°F.

Spread the bread crumbs in a shallow dish. Shape the pork hash into 6 patties. Coat both sides of each with the bread crumbs.

Heat 1 tablespoon of the oil in an ovenproof skillet over medium heat. When hot, cook the patties for 4 to 5 minutes on each side, or until nicely browned and heated through. The patties will sag and loosen. Transfer the skillet to the oven to keep warm.

Bring about 1" of water to a simmer in the bottom of a double boiler over very low heat. Add the remaining 1 tablespoon of oil and the butter in the top of the double boiler. Increase the heat to medium. When the butter melts, add the eggs. Cook the eggs slowly, stirring until they begin to scramble. When they reach a consistency you like, stir in the chives and season to taste with salt and pepper.

To serve, put a hash patty in the center of each of 6 warmed plates. Top with the scrambled eggs.

BEEF HASH *and* POACHED EGGS

Poached eggs are exceedingly healthful because they are cooked without added fat. On the other hand, a lot of their low-fat benefits are lost when served with a crispy hash cake and fried horseradish, but that does not negate the fact that this is a breakfast fit for a king.

I suggest parsnip as a substitute for horseradish root, which is not always easy to find. Parsnips are sweeter than horseradish roots, so the end result will be different but still delicious.

Serves 6

1 TABLESPOON GRAPESEED OIL

6 CUPS UNCOOKED BEEF HASH (PAGE 17)

3 TABLESPOONS FRESH HERBS, SUCH AS THYME LEAVES
   OR FLAT-LEAF PARSLEY

2 TEASPOONS WHITE VINEGAR

6 LARGE EGGS

1 TABLESPOON SLICED FRESH CHIVES

Preheat the oven to 250°F.

Heat the oil in a large ovenproof skillet over medium heat. When hot, cook the hash and herbs for 3 to 4 minutes, or until heated through. Keep warm.

Bring 2 quarts of water and the vinegar to a gentle simmer in a large pot over medium heat.

Add the eggs, one at a time, to the simmering water, swirling the water gently as you drop the eggs into it. Let the eggs poach for 3 to 4 minutes, or until the whites set and the yolks are cooked through and a film forms over them.

Mound the hash in the center of each of 6 warmed plates. Lift the eggs from the water with a slotted spoon. Top each patty with a hot egg. Serve with warm, toasted bread, garnished with reserved horseradish and the chives.

HEIRLOOM POTATO HOME FRIES

What is the great American breakfast without great American home fries? I like to make them with several different kinds and sizes of heirloom potatoes, which I cook separately from each other until they are done. I then finish them in a skillet—a method that ensures that the spuds are perfectly cooked. When you prepare them this way, you can still tell which potatoes are which. In the pan, they get herby, salty, and a little crispy.

Serves 4 to 6

2 POUNDS ASSORTED SMALL HEIRLOOM POTATOES, SUCH AS
    YUKON GOLD, COROLLA, PURPLE PERUVIAN, AND RUBY CRESCENT

1 TEASPOON SEA SALT

¼ CUP EXTRA-VIRGIN OLIVE OIL

4 GARLIC CLOVES, LIGHTLY SMASHED, OR FRESH GARLIC SCAPES

2–4 FRESH WHOLE SAGE LEAVES

2–4 FRESH THYME SPRIGS

2 TABLESPOONS COLD UNSALTED BUTTER, CUT INTO SMALL CUBES

COARSE SEA SALT AND FRESHLY GROUND BLACK PEPPER

Sort the potatoes by size. Put the potatoes, grouped by size, into small saucepans. Cover with water. Bring the water to a simmer over medium-high heat. Add salt until the water tastes like seawater. Cook the potatoes for 12 to 20 minutes, depending on their size and, to some degree, type, or until tender when pierced with the tip of sharp knife. It is better for the potatoes to overcook slightly rather than undercook. When they are done, drain the potatoes and set aside to cool to room temperature.

Heat a large skillet over medium to medium-low heat. When hot, pour 1 tablespoon of the oil into the skillet. Add the garlic or scapes. Cook for 4 to 5 minutes, or until the garlic cloves begin to brown lightly.

Add the remaining oil to the skillet. Halve the cooled potatoes and carefully place them in the skillet so that the cut sides touch the bottom of the pan. Increase the heat to medium. Cook for at least 6 to 8 minutes without disturbing the potatoes. At this point, check to see if they have browned. If they have not browned, cook a little longer.

Using care, turn the potatoes over. Nestle the sage and thyme sprigs between them. Reduce the heat to low and evenly scatter the butter over the potatoes. Cook the potatoes for 4 to 5 minutes longer, or until the butter completely melts into the potatoes and they smell of garlic and fresh herbs.

Sprinkle with salt and pepper and serve hot.

WHOLE GRAIN FRUIT
and VEGETABLE BREAD

Quick breads were once a true staple on American farms and in small-town home kitchens and became an important element of a great American breakfast. These easy loaves are a wonderful way to use healthful whole grains and vegetables because of the moisture and structure these ingredients impart when bound by flour and eggs. The sturdy breads are also fairly indestructible, and slices were often packed in lunch pails or wrapped in napkins and stuffed into jacket pockets to snack on later in the day. They can be used pretty much the same way today. Take a slice to the office or on a road trip, or send it to school with your kids.

This recipe brings together some of the best ingredients of then and of now. If we all were to move forward by glancing back now and then, we might discover or invent some really cool things—not just quick breads—that are truly good for us, our friends, and our environment.

Makes 2 loaves

I CUP SWEET VEGETABLE STOCK OR COMMERCIAL VEGETABLE BROTH

2/3 CUP DRIED CRANBERRIES OR BLUEBERRIES

1/2 VANILLA BEAN OR I TEASPOON PURE VANILLA EXTRACT

I (2 1/2"–3") CANELLA OR CINNAMON STICK

4 LARGE EGGS

2 1/2 CUPS ORGANIC GRANULATED RAW SUGAR

1 1/4 CUPS GRAPESEED OIL + ADDITIONAL FOR OILING PAN

2 1/2 CUPS HARD RED WINTER WHEAT FLOUR OR ANOTHER
   WHOLE WHEAT FLOUR

1 1/2 CUPS ALL-PURPOSE FLOUR

2 TEASPOONS SEA SALT

1 1/2 TEASPOONS BAKING SODA

1/4 TEASPOON BAKING POWDER

2/3 CUP CHOPPED WALNUTS

2 CUPS GRATED ZUCCHINI

I CUP GRATED GOLDEN BEETS OR CARROTS

1/2 CUP COOKED FARRO (PAGE 10) AND 1/2 CUP COOKED
   BLACK BARLEY (PAGE 10) OR I CUP OF EITHER

Combine the vegetable stock, dried fruit, vanilla bean, and canella stick in a saucepan. Bring to a simmer over medium heat. As soon as the mixture simmers, remove from the heat. Set aside to cool to room temperature.

Remove the canella stick and discard. If you used a vanilla bean, scrape the seeds from the bean directly into the cooled stock and discard the pod. Otherwise, add the extract.

Preheat the oven to 325°F. Grease two 8", 9", or 10" loaf pans with oil and lightly dust with flour.

Beat together the eggs and cooled stock at medium-high speed in the bowl of an electric mixer fitted with the paddle attachment until just combined and frothy. Add the sugar and oil. Beat until well combined.

Whisk together the flours, salt, baking soda, and baking powder in another bowl. Stir in the walnuts. Gradually stir the dry ingredients into the beaten eggs, alternating with the zucchini, beets, farro, and barley.

Divide the batter between the loaf pans. Gently tap the pans on the countertop to expel any air bubbles.

Bake for 60 to 70 minutes, rotating the pans once during baking, until a wooden skewer inserted into the middle of each loaf comes out clean. Let the loaves cool in the pans for about 10 minutes. Turn out onto racks. Let the loaves cool completely.

THE STORY OF BAKING SODA

I LOVE HOW HISTORY OFFERS EXAMPLES OF "WASTE" TURNED INTO SOMETHING POSITIVE. BAKING SODA, WHICH LEAVENS QUICK BREADS, IS A GOOD EXAMPLE. ITS FIRST KNOWN USE WAS BY NATIVE AMERICANS TO REMOVE THE OUTER HULLS FROM CORN KERNELS (HOMINY), BUT PEARL ASH (AKA POT ASH OR SODA) WAS QUICKLY DISCOVERED TO BE AN EFFECTIVE LEAVENING AGENT, LIKELY BY HAPPY ACCIDENT. PEARL ASH GAINED POPULARITY AS A LEAVENING AGENT IN THE 18TH CENTURY, NOT COINCIDENTALLY WHEN QUICK BREADS MADE THEIR APPEARANCE.

FRENCH TOAST *with* BROWN SUGAR BANANAS

If you are one of those people who just loves French toast, try this gussied-up version.
I recommend you use the Old-Fashioned Honey-Wheat Bread on page 12, a good egg bread,
or any substantial loaf. French toast is a good way to use day-old or slightly stale bread.
This is wonderful for a weekend breakfast or brunch.

Serves 8

- 3–4 TABLESPOONS GRAPESEED OIL
- 4 LARGE EGGS, LIGHTLY BEATEN
- ⅔ CUP MILK
- SEEDS FROM ½ VANILLA BEAN OR ½ TEASPOON PURE VANILLA EXTRACT
- 2 TABLESPOONS LOCAL HONEY
- ¼ TEASPOON KOSHER SALT
- ¼ TEASPOON FRESHLY GROUND BLACK PEPPER
- 8 SLICES RICH EGG BREAD, SUCH AS CHALLAH OR BRIOCHE, EACH ABOUT ¾" THICK
- 4 BANANAS, PEELED AND HALVED LENGTHWISE
- ¼ CUP RAW GRANULATED SUGAR
- 8 SCOOPS VANILLA ICE CREAM OR YOUR FAVORITE FLAVOR
- ¼ CUP MAPLE SYRUP
- FRESH CURRANTS, FOR GARNISH (OPTIONAL)

Preheat the broiler to high. Set the top rack as close as possible to the heating element.

Heat half of the oil in a heavy-bottomed skillet over medium heat.

Meanwhile, stir together the eggs, milk, vanilla bean, honey, salt, and pepper in a wide, 3"-deep baking dish. Submerge or dip 4 slices of bread into the seasoned egg mixture for 30 seconds. Drain on a plate for about 1 minute. Cook in the skillet for about 3 minutes on each side, or until crisp and lightly browned. Transfer to a warm platter. Add the remaining oil. Repeat the process with the remaining slices of bread.

Arrange the banana halves on a baking sheet, cut side up. Evenly sprinkle the sugar over the bananas. Broil until the sugar melts and turns crisp.

Put a slice of French toast in the center of each of 8 warmed plates. Top with the ice cream. Put a glazed banana slice on each piece of toast next to the ice cream. Drizzle with the maple syrup.

BREAKFAST PORRIDGE

Before cereal grains were turned into "cereal," they were known only as the seeds of very large grass plants. These plants constituted one of the first successful forms of agriculture, and early farmers could gaze across fields of tall grass weighted down with heads of ripe grains and rest easy in the knowledge that the seeds translated into food. Thankfully, man has always had an innate desire to make food taste good, so we developed cooking methods for these seeds that often also included fresh or dried fruits, berries, vegetables, and roasted nuts, all of which added texture, flavor, and substance while the nuts—by luck or design—added extra protein.

This recipe reflects the whole shooting match, with grains, fruits, and nuts. It tastes best when the dried fruits and berries are stirred into the porridge 5 to 10 minutes before serving. This helps cool the porridge while rehydrating the fruit, and its flavor infuses the cooked grains. Add the nuts at the end to preserve the crunchiness. Downright delicious!

Serves 2 or 3

3 cups water

1 teaspoon sea salt

1 cup steel-cut oats

2 tablespoons butter

1½ cups whole milk

2 cups Cooked Farro or spelt (page 10)

2 cups Cooked Black Barley (page 10)

½ cup dried cranberries

½ cup dried blueberries

¼ cup roasted almonds or pistachios

Plain yogurt (optional)

Buttermilk (optional)

Local honey or agave syrup (optional)

Bring the water to a boil over high heat in a large saucepan. When boiling, add the salt and then the oats and cook for about 5 minutes, stirring constantly, until the porridge reaches first starch. This is when the oats are suspended in the liquid.

Add the butter, reduce the heat to medium, and simmer for about 15 minutes, stirring occasionally, until the porridge thickens. Adjust the heat up or down to maintain the simmer.

Gently stir in the milk and simmer for about 20 minutes longer. Stir in the cooked grains and cook just until heated through. Stir in the cranberries and blueberries, remove the pan from the heat, and let the porridge sit for about 5 minutes. Stir in the nuts and serve. If desired, stir in yogurt or buttermilk and honey or agave syrup.

HEIRLOOM GRAINS

HEIRLOOM GRAINS ARE VARIETIES THAT HAVE NEVER BEEN MODIFIED AND THAT HAVE BEEN PASSED DOWN THROUGH THE GENERATIONS. UNFORTUNATELY, THEY ARE DIFFICULT TO FIND IN MANY SUPERMARKETS, WHICH TEND TO PRIORITIZE SHELF LIFE OVER NUTRITION.

I LOVE ALL ANCIENT GRAINS, ESPECIALLY FARRO PICCOLO, THE OLDEST CULTIVATED VARIETY OF FARRO, FOR ITS LIGHT, NUTTY FLAVOR AND HIGH NUTRITIONAL VALUE. THERE ARE ALMOST TOO MANY OF THESE GRAINS TO COUNT, BUT TO NAME A FEW OF THOSE MORE COMMONLY AVAILABLE, THERE ARE BLACK BARLEY, QUINOA, SPELT, AND GRANO (WHICH IS THE WHOLE SEED HEAD OF SEMOLINA).

ALL VARIETIES BENEFIT FROM SLOW, GENTLE SIMMERING AND A LIGHT SPRINKLE OF SEA SALT ONCE COOKED. THESE DELICIOUS GRAINS CAN BE USED IN ANY NUMBER OF RECIPES, FROM BREAKFAST PORRIDGE TO RISOTTO. "AFTER ALL, THE ORIGINAL RISOTTO WAS MADE USING FARRO." TURN TO PAGE 227 TO DISCOVER WHERE TO ORDER THESE GRAINS.

Chapter 3

SOUPS, SALADS, AND SMALL PLATES

It can be argued that soups are the fuel that fed our growing nation in its earliest years. In the days when food was cooked continually in the home kitchen—those long-ago times before take-out and frozen dinners—stocks and broths were always accessible, so soups were easy to make. Whether simmering on the crane arm over a kitchen hearth, on the back of a coal-fed stove, or in the pot set over a western-moving wagon train's campfire, soups and their close cousins, stews, were always satisfying and generally easy to make. Plus, both were and still are an excellent way to stretch a family budget or feed many. No one would argue that the lunch-box thermos was invented as a way for miners, farmers, and other laborers to carry hot soup with them on the job and for schoolchildren to take it for lunch.

These days, I see an opportunity for getting homemade soup—rather than canned— back into the kitchen and onto our tables. Once you start making soup, you will be amazed at how easy it is. Soups utilize just about anything you have in the pantry, last a long time in the refrigerator and longer in the freezer, and transport well to school and the office. And like so many of the dishes in this book, they fill the house with incredible aromas as they cook.

Really, who objects to a bowl of soup? I have met people who don't like sweet potatoes, who disdain grits, and who avoid fish—but never anyone who turns down a bowl of soup.

CHICKEN NOODLE SOUP

TOMATO RICE SOUP WITH BRAISED BEEF SHANKS

TOMATO SOUP WITH GRILLED CHEESE GARNISH

AUTUMN SQUASH AND HEIRLOOM BEAN SOUP

PARSNIP SOUP

NATIVE CORN AND SUNCHOKE CHOWDER

(continued)

Sweet Pea Soup

Garden Gazpacho

Sweet Corn Chowder

She-Crab Soup

Nantucket Scallop Porridge with Apples
and Chestnuts

"Use a Spoon" Chopped Salad

Heirloom Beet Salad with Savory Marshmallows

Watermelon and Arugula Salad

Candied Quince, Pear, and Goat Cheese Tart

Chicken Liver Mousse

Onion-Thyme Flatbread

CHICKEN NOODLE SOUP

Although you can make this soup with any good chicken stock you have on hand—preferably one you have made yourself—the delight of this recipe is that it is self-contained.

My coauthor, Mary, learned to make broth this way when she worked with Edna Lewis on her book, In Pursuit of Flavor, *and I love the technique. Miss Lewis, as she was always called, was one of America's greatest cooks, and in her quiet way, she influenced many of us who came after. Born in 1916 in Freetown, Virginia, the granddaughter of freed slaves, she learned to cook with the bounty of the local harvest and she never compromised her strong convictions to use only the freshest and purest ingredients available. Nor did she compromise on the genuine hospitality with which such great food should be served.*

This simple chicken soup is an example of how something fairly "everyday" can, with just a little care, make a hero out of anyone.

Serves 4

1 (3–3½-POUND) CHICKEN

SEA SALT

1 LARGE ONION, CHOPPED

5–6 FRESH THYME SPRIGS

4 CUPS WATER

2½ OUNCES EGG NOODLES

FRESHLY GROUND BLACK PEPPER

Cut the chicken into 10 to 12 pieces using a sharp knife or poultry shears. Salt them lightly.

Heat a 4- or 5-quart saucepan or Dutch oven with a tight-fitting lid over high heat. When hot, put the chicken pieces and onion in the pot and stir constantly for about 5 minutes to sear the chicken on both sides. Add the thyme, cover the pan tightly, and reduce the heat to low. Let the chicken cook undisturbed for about 20 minutes. At this point, the chicken will have released enough liquid to nearly cover the chicken pieces. If not, cook for another 5 minutes.

Add the water to the pot and bring to a boil over medium-high heat. Reduce the heat to low and simmer very gently for 20 minutes. Drain the chicken broth into another pot or a bowl and set it and the chicken aside to cool. When the chicken is cool enough to handle, pull the meat from the bones, discarding the bones and skin. Tear or cut the meat into bite-size pieces.

Skim the fat off the surface of the broth. Return the defatted broth to the pan and add more water if you don't have 5 to 5½ cups. Add the egg noodles, bring to a boil over high heat, reduce the heat to medium, and cook for about 5 minutes, or until softened. Add the chicken. Cook for about 5 minutes longer, or until the noodles are tender. Remove the thyme sprigs, if desired. Season to taste with salt and pepper and serve hot.

TOMATO RICE SOUP
with BRAISED BEEF SHANKS

When I first met Lori, she had me convinced me she was something of a foodie—until I found out she couldn't cook her way out of a paper bag! So imagine my surprise when I came home one night to an apartment building that smelled amazing and realized that the delicious aroma was emanating from our place. Lori had cooked her grandpa's Polish soup as a surprise and because she couldn't go through another Milwaukee winter without it. After 1 spoonful, I understood why. Since those days, Lori has become a very fine cook. She still makes this thick, earthy, intensely flavored soup that her Polish-born grandfather passed on to his daughter, who passed it on to Lori. Our kids love it, and now our daughter Courtney makes it all the time—talk about an heirloom recipe!

Until I tasted this, I had not considered making soup with beef shanks. They are sold in slices with a center marrow bone. I suggest you return the marrow bone to the pot after you cut the meat from it. It's a gift that keeps on giving in terms of flavor.

Serves 8

2 TABLESPOONS GRAPESEED OIL

2 BONE-IN BEEF SHANK SLICES, EACH 12 OUNCES AND ABOUT 1" THICK

KOSHER SALT AND FRESHLY GROUND BLACK PEPPER

1 POUND CUBED BEEF STEW MEAT, SUCH AS SHOULDER OR BLADE ROAST

2–3 CELERY RIBS, CUT INTO 1/4"–1/2"-THICK SLICES

1–2 LARGE CARROTS, PEELED AND CUT INTO ABOUT 1/4"–1/2"-THICK SLICES

1 ONION, DICED

1 GARLIC CLOVE, CRUSHED

1 QUART BEEF OR CHICKEN STOCK

1 FRESH BAY LEAF

1 QUART TOMATO JUICE

1/2 CUP BROWN RICE

1 1/2 CUPS WATER

1 CUP MILK OR SOUR CREAM, AT ROOM TEMPERATURE

Heat the oil in a large stockpot over medium-high heat. When the oil is hot enough to ripple, season the beef shanks on both sides with salt and pepper, and sear for about 6 minutes on each side, or until nicely browned. Remove the shanks from the pot and set aside, covered, to keep warm.

Season the stew meat with salt and pepper and cook, stirring, for about 6 minutes, or until well browned all over. Remove the meat from the pot and set aside.

Add the celery and carrots to the pot, reduce the heat to medium, and cook for 3 to 4 minutes, or until the vegetables are lightly browned and have released some liquid. Add the onion and garlic and cook for 3 to 4 minutes longer, or until lightly browned.

Return the stew meat and beef shanks to the pot. Add the stock and bay leaf, bring to a simmer over medium-high heat, partially cover, reduce the heat to low, and simmer gently for $1\frac{1}{2}$ hours. Turn the heat off beneath the pot.

Lift the shanks from the pot and transfer to a cutting board. Cut the meat off the bone into bite-size pieces, trimming any fat or gristle. Return the meat and marrow bones to the pot.

Add the tomato juice. Return to a simmer over medium-high heat and cook gently for 30 minutes. Add the rice and water and cook over medium heat for 45 to 55 minutes, or until the rice is cooked through and tender.

Season to taste with salt and pepper. Stir in the milk until well blended. Serve immediately.

TOMATO SOUP *with* GRILLED CHEESE GARNISH

Ironically enough, my mom's maiden name was Campbell, and this soup is the staple soup we ate as kids—we joked about the coincidence every time she ladled it into bowls. Of course, this is freshly made, not from a can. Of course, I recommend making this when the tomatoes are at their very best; otherwise, use your own put-ups (page 22) or good canned tomatoes. Serving it with a grilled cheese sandwich just makes sense. Who doesn't love this combo?

Serves 6 to 8

Soup

6–8 ripe tomatoes, cored and cut into wedges, or canned tomatoes, drained and cut into wedges

2 cups extra-virgin olive oil

2 cups scalded milk

½ cup sliced fresh basil (1 bunch), packed

Kosher salt and freshly ground black pepper

Sandwich

8 ounces soft Brie or Camembert

16 thick slices sourdough ficelle, cut on a sharp bias

½ cup (1 stick) unsalted butter, softened

Preheat the oven to 150°F.

Put the tomatoes in a baking dish just large enough to hold them in 1 layer. Pour the oil over them to coat all the wedges evenly. Roast the tomatoes for 4 hours, or until they are fully wilted. If possible, leave them in the oven for twice the time—or overnight—for the best result.

Transfer the tomatoes, oil, and accumulated juices to a large saucepan. Bring to a simmer over medium heat. As soon as the tomatoes simmer, lift them from the oil with a spoon (you want some of the oil and juices, although not all) and transfer to a blender or food processor. Add some of the oil and juices, depending on your taste preference. Blend in batches while slowly adding the scalded milk and basil. Season to taste with salt and pepper. Set aside and keep warm.

Evenly distribute the cheese among 8 slices of bread. Top with the remaining slices of bread to form cheese sandwiches. Butter the top and bottom of each sandwich.

Meanwhile, heat a heavy-bottomed skillet over medium heat. Cook the sandwiches for about 2 minutes on each side, or until lightly browned and the cheese is melted.

Ladle the soup into bowls and serve the cheese sandwiches alongside.

AUTUMN SQUASH
and HEIRLOOM BEAN SOUP

Hard squash and beans are two components of what Native Americans and other proponents of Native American farming call Three Sisters' agriculture. The third component is corn. When grown together, the three crops help each other flourish and represent one of the best examples of companion planting. Native cultures have cooked these foods, all of which are indigenous to the Western Hemisphere, for centuries. I celebrate the relationship between beans and hard squash in this simple soup and jazz them up with a little hot chile pepper, another integral part of Native American cooking.

Serves 6

2 POUNDS HARD SQUASH, SUCH AS BUTTERCUP, KABOCHA, RED CURRY, BUTTERNUT, OR OTHER HEIRLOOM SQUASH, PEELED, SEEDED, AND CUT INTO 1" CUBES

3 TABLESPOONS GRAPESEED OIL

KOSHER SALT AND FRESHLY GROUND BLACK PEPPER

1 TABLESPOON UNSALTED BUTTER

1 SWEET ONION, CUT ROOT TO STEM END INTO ¼"-THICK SLICES

6 GARLIC CLOVES, HALVED LENGTHWISE

2 CUPS KALE OR OTHER HEARTY WINTER GREEN

½ SMALL RED THAI OR JALAPEÑO CHILE PEPPER, SEEDED AND FINELY SLICED

4 CUPS VEGETABLE OR CHICKEN STOCK, PREFERABLY HOMEMADE

3 CUPS COOKED DRIED HEIRLOOM BEANS (PAGE 8) SUCH AS CRANBERRY, INDIAN WOMAN, LIMA, OR TIGER'S EYE

1 TABLESPOON FRESH OREGANO, MARJORAM, OR SAGE

Preheat the oven to 350°F.

Toss the squash cubes with 2 tablespoons of the oil in a large bowl. Add salt and black pepper to taste. Spread the squash evenly on a baking sheet and roast for about 25 minutes, or until the squash is nearly tender when pierced with a fork.

Meanwhile, heat the remaining 1 tablespoon of oil in a skillet over medium heat. Add the butter. When it melts, add the onion and cook, stirring occasionally, for about 8 minutes, or until the onion softens and begins to brown. Add the garlic and cook, stirring continually, for about 8 minutes longer, or until the garlic is lightly browned and softened. Add the kale and cook for about 3 minutes, or until the greens begin to wilt.

(continued)

Transfer two-thirds of the cooked squash to a large saucepan and add the chile pepper and stock. Set the remaining squash cubes aside and cover to keep warm. Bring the stock to a simmer over medium heat, reduce the heat, partially cover, and simmer for 20 to 25 minutes, or until the squash is soft enough to puree. Adjust the heat to maintain the simmer.

Transfer the squash and stock to a blender or food processor and blend until smooth. You will have to do this in batches. Alternatively, use an immersion blender to puree the soup directly in the pot. Return the blended soup to the pan and stir in the reserved squash cubes, onion, garlic, cooked beans, and kale. Stir in the oregano and cook for about 5 minutes, or until the flavors develop fully. Season to taste with salt and black pepper and serve.

PARSNIP SOUP

Parsnips are great in the fall, which is when we are most likely to use them, but spring parsnips are remarkable. They tend to be a little sweeter than their autumn cousins because when they sprout in the spring, they are full of the sugar that has been stored in the root under the frozen winter ground. If you are lucky enough to find spring parsnips, make this soup immediately. You will be rewarded. And yet it's excellent with fall parsnips, too. I like to mix yogurt and sour cream for a tangy balance of flavors, enhanced only by a good grind of pepper. If you can, use thick Greek yogurt, and if you find goat's milk yogurt, better still!

Serves 4; makes about 1½ quarts

2 TABLESPOONS GRAPESEED OIL

8 PARSNIPS, PEELED AND HALVED LENGTHWISE

1 QUART WATER

½ CUP PLAIN GREEK YOGURT

¼ CUP SOUR CREAM

KOSHER SALT AND FRESHLY GROUND BLACK PEPPER

2–3 TABLESPOONS CHOPPED FRESH TARRAGON

Preheat the oven to 375°F. Lightly oil a shallow roasting pan with 1 tablespoon of the oil.

Rub the parsnip pieces with the remaining 1 tablespoon of oil. Put the parsnip halves, cut side down, in the pan. Cover tightly with foil or a lid and roast for about 45 minutes, or until the parsnips are fully cooked and well browned on the cut sides. Don't worry if some of the parsnips are very browned; these will taste great in the soup.

Transfer the parsnips to a cutting board. Reserve half. Push a knife through the remainder to break them into smaller pieces. You will have about 2½ cups of parsnip pieces.

Meanwhile, bring the water to a simmer in a large stockpot set over medium-high heat. Put the chopped parsnips in the simmering water and cook for 10 to 15 minutes, or until the parsnips are tender when pierced with a fork. Transfer to a blender and puree until smooth.
You will have to do this in batches. Return the soup to the pot. Alternatively, use an immersion blender to puree the soup directly in the pan.

Cut the reserved parsnips into bite-size pieces. Add to the stockpot and bring to a simmer just to heat through.

As soon as the soup simmers, remove it from the heat and stir in the yogurt and sour cream. Season to taste with salt and pepper. Stir in the tarragon. Serve immediately.

NATIVE CORN
and SUNCHOKE CHOWDER

The corn in this soup is hominy, which is what the early settlers called native corn that was cooked as the Native Americans cooked it—with a little pot ash. The pot ash softened the hull of the corn so it could be removed, and in the process it made the protein in the corn more digestible and nutritious. When you first cook hominy, don't be concerned when the corn splits open and "blooms." This is meant to happen, so hominy resembles wet popcorn and tastes like meaty, tender corn chips.

The hominy tastes great with sunchokes, also called Jerusalem artichokes, which are the tubers of small, indigenous American sunflowers. Sunflowers were grown by Native Americans as agriculture, not horticulture. They thrive in northern and southern climates and are pest resistant. And did I mention that they are delicious too? Put these two together for a tasty and fortifying soup. You can order hominy from Anson Mills.

Serves 8 to 10

- 2 cups yellow hominy (I like Anson Mills Henry Moore hominy)
- 2 tablespoons grapeseed oil
- 1–2 carrots, coarsely chopped
- 1 onion, coarsely chopped
- 1 medium to large parsnip, peeled and coarsely chopped
- 4 cups sunchokes (about 1½ pounds), peeled and coarsely chopped
- Kosher salt and freshly ground black pepper
- ½ cup coarsely chopped mixed fresh herbs, such as thyme, rosemary, parsley, savory, and chives

Put the hominy in a large bowl and pour enough water over the hominy to cover it generously. Set aside to soak for at least 8 hours and up to 12. Drain.

Combine the drained hominy and 2 quarts of water in a stockpot. Bring to a simmer over medium heat. Reduce the heat to medium-low so that the water barely simmers and cook, partially covered, for 2 to 2½ hours, or until the hominy is soft and blooms, something like popcorn. If the cooking liquid evaporates so that its level is below the grain, add ½ to 1 cup of water. Drain the hominy and reserve the cooking liquid. You will have about 5 cups of liquid and 8 cups of hominy.

Wipe out the stockpot. Add the oil, carrots, onion, and parsnip. Cook over medium heat, stirring, for 3 to 4 minutes, or until the vegetables are heated through and very shiny.

Add the hominy cooking liquid and enough extra water to equal 8 cups and the sunchokes to the pot. Bring to a simmer over medium heat. Cook for 10 to 15 minutes, or until the vegetables are cooked through.

Remove about half of the vegetables from the stock using a handled strainer or a large slotted spoon. Set them aside. Continue to cook the remaining vegetables for 3 to 5 minutes longer, or until they break apart when stirred.

Transfer the reserved vegetables and some of the cooking liquid to a blender or the bowl of a food processor fitted with a metal blade and blend until smooth. You may have to do this in batches.

Return the blended vegetables to the pot with the reserved hominy and vegetables. Bring to a simmer and season to taste with salt and pepper.

To serve, ladle into warmed bowls and top with the mixed herbs.

SWEET PEA SOUP

Although many of us think of the rich, hearty soup made with dried split peas when we hear the phrase "pea soup," a soup made with fresh sweet peas is lovely. I like to make this with shelled peas straight from the garden; good-quality, organic frozen peas do in a pinch.

I use potatoes to thicken the soup. Thickening with cornstarch, arrowroot, or a floury roux can interfere with the flavor of the soup, while a potato is less obtrusive. Chilling the peas accomplishes the same thing as shocking them in ice water to keep their color bright. I prefer the freezer method, as the flavor of the peas is not "shocked" out of them.

Serves 4 to 6; makes about 2 quarts

- ½ pound Yukon gold potatoes (1 or 2 potatoes)
- 6 cups vegetable stock, preferably homemade
- 2 tablespoons grapeseed oil
- 1 cup diced onion
- 4 cups shelled sweet peas (from about 4 pounds in the pod) or frozen organic peas
- 2–3 tablespoons thinly sliced fresh mint or Thai basil
- Kosher salt and freshly ground black pepper
- 3–4 tablespoons softened unsalted butter

Put a rimmed baking sheet in the freezer to chill.

Cover the potatoes with a generous amount of water in a saucepan. Bring to a boil over medium-high heat. Reduce the heat to medium and simmer briskly for 15 to 20 minutes, or until the potatoes are tender but not mushy. Drain the potatoes. When cool enough to handle, peel and cut the potatoes into 1" cubes. You should have about 1 cup of cubed potatoes.

Meanwhile, heat the oil and onion in a large skillet over medium heat. Cook for 8 to 10 minutes, or until the onions caramelize lightly. Add the fresh peas and cook for 5 to 6 minutes, or until just cooked through. If using frozen peas, heat them just until the soup is hot. Immediately transfer the onion and peas to the chilled baking sheet. Place them in the freezer for 8 to 10 minutes, or until the peas are cold.

In a 3-quart or larger saucepan, bring the stock to a simmer over medium-high heat. Add the cold onion and peas and the cubed potatoes to the hot stock. Bring the soup to a simmer over medium-high heat. When the soup simmers and is heated through, transfer the soup to a blender and process until very smooth. You will have to do this in batches. Alternatively, use an immersion blender to puree the soup directly in the pan.

Return the soup to the pot and add the mint or basil. Season to taste with salt and pepper. Stir in the butter. Serve immediately, or strain through a fine-mesh sieve for a more refined soup and garnish with additional mint or basil leaves.

GARDEN GAZPACHO

When our garden is bursting with summer's bounty, Lori and I have been known to look at each other with bewilderment and awe. How can we possibly pick everything that is ready? How can we prepare it all? Over the years, we have stopped thinking "salad" or "ratatouille" at these times. Instead we think "blender!" and "gazpacho!"

Is there a bad combination of vegetables for gazpacho? I don't think so. There is traditional gazpacho bursting with the goodness of summer tomatoes and red onions; white gazpacho made with turnips, cucumbers, and jicama; and yellow gazpacho rife with yellow peppers, orange tomatoes, banana peppers, and golden beets. All gazpachos love alliums: onions, chives, and garlic. They all love herbs, from mint and basil to dill. They even accept vegetables that need cooking, such as mushrooms and eggplant (chilled before adding, of course). In short, you can take almost any vegetable from the garden and toss it in the blender or food processor and end up with a cold soup.

Serves 8 to 10

PUREE

3 CUPS SAVORY VEGETABLE STOCK (PAGE 20)

1 CUP DRAINED PUT-UP TOMATOES (PAGE 22) OR AN EQUAL AMOUNT
OF CHOPPED FRESH TOMATOES

$\frac{1}{2}$ CUP ORGANIC GRAPEFRUIT SEGMENTS (NO WHITE MEMBRANES),
FINELY CHOPPED (ABOUT $\frac{1}{2}$ GRAPEFRUIT)

1 ORGANIC AVOCADO, PEELED, PIT REMOVED, AND COARSELY CHOPPED

2 TABLESPOONS FRESH LIME JUICE

2 TABLESPOONS SLIGHTLY SWEET RED WINE VINEGAR, SUCH AS
ONE MADE FROM SYRAH OR PINOT NOIR GRAPES

SEA SALT AND FRESHLY GROUND BLACK PEPPER

SOUP

6 MEDIUM TO LARGE RIPE HEIRLOOM TOMATOES, PEELED, SEEDED,
AND CHOPPED

6 GARLIC CLOVES, SMASHED VIGOROUSLY WITH SEA SALT (SEE NOTE)

2 RED BELL PEPPERS, SEEDED AND DICED

1 LARGE CUCUMBER OR 2–3 SMALL CUCUMBERS, PEELED, SEEDED,
AND DICED

1 RED ONION, DICED

1 JALAPEÑO OR SERRANO CHILE PEPPER, SEEDED AND FINELY DICED
  (WEAR PLASTIC GLOVES WHEN HANDLING)

1 YELLOW BANANA PEPPER, FINELY DICED

3 CUPS SAVORY VEGETABLE STOCK (PAGE 20)

1 CUP CANNED TOMATOES, DRAINED

1/2 CUP ORGANIC GRAPEFRUIT SEGMENTS, FINELY CHOPPED

1/4 CUP CHOPPED FRESH CILANTRO

1/4 CUP FINELY SLICED FRESH CHERVIL

1/4 CUP FINELY SLICED FRESH BASIL

2 TABLESPOONS FRESH LIME JUICE

1/3 CUP EXTRA-VIRGIN OLIVE OIL

SEA SALT AND FRESHLY GROUND BLACK PEPPER

To make the puree: Combine the stock, tomatoes, grapefruit, avocado, lime juice, and vinegar in a blender and process until smooth. You may have to do this in batches. Season to taste with sea salt and pepper and set aside.

To make the soup: Toss together the heirloom tomatoes, garlic, bell peppers, cucumber, onion, chile pepper, banana pepper, stock, canned tomatoes, grapefruit, cilantro, chervil, basil, and lime juice in a large glass, ceramic, or other nonreactive bowl. Stir in the puree and half of the olive oil. Adjust the seasoning with salt and pepper.

Serve drizzled with the remaining oil.

Note: TO SMASH THE GARLIC, LAY THE CLOVES ON A CUTTING BOARD, SPRINKLE WITH SALT, AND USE THE FLAT SIDE OF A CHEF'S KNIFE TO SMASH THEM. OR PUT THE CLOVES IN A MORTAR, SPRINKLE WITH SALT, AND SMASH LIGHTLY WITH A PESTLE.

SWEET CORN CHOWDER

Over the years, we have come to value sweet corn as a special summertime treat. The best summer corn is not the silvery white stuff that tastes like sugar with only a hint of corn, rather than the other way around, but the yellow ears. These taste more of corn, and although they are disappearing in favor of sweeter varieties, they are important (though not critical) to this recipe. I juice the raw kernels to add to soup as a thickening agent. I believe the yellow kernels do this most successfully, so you will need a juicer for this recipe. Whichever kind of corn you use, you are in for a treat with this chowder.

Serves 6 to 8

20 EARS SWEET CORN, SHUCKED

¼ CUP GRAPESEED OIL + MORE FOR BRUSHING ON CORN

1 LARGE YUKON GOLD OR OTHER HEIRLOOM POTATO

2 CARROTS, DICED

1 ONION, DICED

4 OUNCES CELERY ROOT, PEELED AND DICED

1 QUART SAVORY VEGETABLE STOCK (PAGE 20)

2 TABLESPOONS FINELY CHOPPED FRESH TARRAGON

2 TABLESPOONS THINLY CHOPPED FLAT-LEAF PARSLEY

2 TABLESPOONS UNSALTED BUTTER, AT ROOM TEMPERATURE

2 TABLESPOONS GOAT'S MILK YOGURT OR ANY HIGH-QUALITY
    COW'S MILK YOGURT, AT ROOM TEMPERATURE

KOSHER SALT AND FRESHLY GROUND BLACK PEPPER

Preheat the oven to 400°F.

Brush 10 ears of the corn with oil. Place on a baking sheet and roast, turning once or twice, for about 45 minutes, or until the kernels are slightly browned on at least 2 sides. Set aside to cool.

Put the potato in a saucepan with enough cold water to cover by about 1". Bring to a boil and cook for about 20 minutes, or until the potato is tender when pierced with a fork. Drain and let the potato cool. Cut in half and set aside.

Heat the ¼ cup of oil in a large stockpot over medium-high heat. When hot, cook the carrots for 4 to 6 minutes, or until they begin to soften. Add the onion and celery root and cook for about 5 minutes longer, or until the onions are translucent and lightly browned. Cover and set aside.

With a sharp kitchen knife, cut the roasted kernels from the cobs and add them to the pot with the other vegetables.

With the same knife, cut the uncooked kernels from the remaining 10 cobs. Run the raw kernels through a vegetable juicer and set the juice aside.

Heat the stock in a large saucepan over medium-high heat until simmering. Transfer half of the stock to a blender and add one potato half. Blend until smooth. Pour the thickened stock into a bowl and put the rest of the stock and the remaining potato half into the blender and puree. Add this to the rest of the thickened stock.

Remove the lid from the stockpot and pour the slightly thickened stock over the vegetables. Add the sweet corn juice, making sure any cornstarch settled on the bottom of the container gets into the soup. Bring the soup to a simmer over medium heat. Immediately reduce the heat to medium-low and simmer very gently for about 5 minutes.

Stir in the tarragon and parsley. Remove the soup from the heat. Swirl in the butter and yogurt. Adjust the seasoning with salt and pepper and serve hot.

CORN: A NATIONAL TREASURE

IF I WERE ASKED TO NAME A NATIONAL VEGETABLE, I WOULD SINGLE OUT CORN. WITHOUT CORN, THE JAMESTOWN SETTLERS WOULD HAVE PERISHED, AS THEY NEARLY DID WHEN THE ALGONQUIN WITHHELD THE VITAL FOODSTUFF AS PART OF THE ONGOING FEUD BETWEEN THE NATIVE AMERICANS AND THE COLONISTS. LUCKILY, THE ENGLISH MAINTAINED RELATIONS WITH THE POWHATAN TRIBES AND SO WERE ABLE TO TRADE FOR CORN, VENISON, AND FISH.

DURING THESE EARLY DAYS, NATIVE FARMERS CROSSED SWEET CORN WITH GRINDING CORN TO PRODUCE THE VERY BEST COOKING CORN, REFERRED TO BY THE COLONISTS AS HOMINY. THIS WOULD NOT THE ÜBER-HYBRIDIZED, GENETICALLY MODIFIED FRANKENCORN WE KNOW TODAY BUT, RATHER, FLINT CORN, HOMINY, AND NATIVE SWEET CORN, THE KIND OF CORN THAT HAS COVERED SMALL PATCHES OF OUR COUNTRYSIDE SINCE LONG BEFORE THE ENGLISH ARRIVED.

ALTHOUGH CORN IS OFFICIALLY A GRAIN, WE THINK OF IT AS A VEGETABLE. LIKE OUR NATIONAL BIRD, THE BALD EAGLE, IT IS STRONG AND MAJESTIC, ITS GOLDEN KERNELS BEAUTIFUL TO BEHOLD. LIKE THE WILD TURKEY, WHICH BENJAMIN FRANKLIN CHAMPIONED AS THE NATIONAL BIRD OF THE UNITED STATES, CORN IS RESPONSIBLE FOR SUSTAINING OUR GROWING NATION.

SHE-CRAB SOUP

She-crab soup is the clam chowder of the South, and just as we have all experienced lousy clam chowder, it's not unusual to have mediocre-to-poor she-crab soup. But, take my word for it, when you sample a really good she-crab soup, it blows you away.

Enjoy this soup as often as you can during crab season (early to late spring through fall) and dream about it the rest of the year. This gives the crabs time to reproduce and replenish, which is only fair and good stewardship of our waters.

Serves 8

4 TABLESPOONS UNSALTED BUTTER

¼ CUP DICED ONION OR SHALLOT

2 TABLESPOONS FLOUR

1 QUART MILK, SCALDED

2½ CUPS HEAVY CREAM

½ TEASPOON FRESHLY GRATED NUTMEG

2 POUNDS WHITE JUMBO LUMP FEMALE BLUE CRABMEAT WITH ROE (ABOUT 4 CUPS)

4 HARD-COOKED EGG YOLKS, GRATED OR MASHED WITH A FORK

KOSHER SALT AND FRESHLY GROUND BLACK PEPPER

4–6 TABLESPOONS VERY GOOD DRY SHERRY

3 TABLESPOONS SLICED FRESH CHIVES

Heat 1 tablespoon of the butter in a small skillet over medium heat. When hot, add the onion and cook for 3 to 4 minutes, or until translucent. Set aside.

Prepare a large double boiler or a large pan set over another pot holding water. Bring the water in the base to a low simmer over medium-low heat. Set the top of the double boiler over the simmering water and melt the remaining 3 tablespoons of butter. Stir in the flour until mixed with the butter and cook for 5 to 7 minutes, or until the roux is smooth.

Stirring constantly, add the scalded milk and 2 cups of the cream to the pan until well mixed and the liquid is slightly thickened by the roux. Stir in the reserved onion and the nutmeg. Add the crabmeat and roe. Simmer for about 20 minutes, stirring gently now and then.

While the soup simmers, whip the remaining ½ cup of cream to firm but not stiff peaks.

Stir the egg yolks and whipped cream into the crab soup until just incorporated.

Meanwhile, warm the sherry until just lukewarm in a small pot over low heat. Spoon the sherry into each of 8 soup bowls, dividing it evenly. Ladle the soup over the sherry, garnish with the chives, and serve immediately.

NANTUCKET SCALLOP PORRIDGE *with* APPLES *and* CHESTNUTS

Here I pair sweet scallops with ancient grains and barley. These grains have very low environmental impact and are notably healthful, and when you cook with them, you support multiculture farming. The method is similar to making a risotto, but I have dubbed it porridge, a good New England word to go with New England scallops. The flavors are wonderful.

Serves 4

4 TABLESPOONS GRAPESEED OIL

¼ CUP DICED ONION

½ CUP PEELED AND DICED (ABOUT ¼") HEIRLOOM SQUASH,
    SUCH AS KABOCHA, BUTTERCUP, OR BUTTERNUT

1 CUP PEELED AND DICED (¼" PIECES) ROASTED CHESTNUTS
    (SEE NOTE ON PAGE 182)

1 CUP COOKED BLACK BARLEY OR FARRO (PAGE 10) OR 1 CUP
    COOKED GRANO OR SPELT

1 CUP RICH CHICKEN STOCK, PREFERABLY HOMEMADE

½ CUP FRESH APPLE CIDER

½ CUP PEELED AND DICED GOOD-QUALITY BAKING APPLE,
    SUCH AS REAL GRANNY SMITH OR PIPPIN

½ CUP CRÈME FRAÎCHE OR SOUR CREAM

KOSHER SALT AND FRESHLY GROUND BLACK PEPPER

3 CUPS FRESH BAY SCALLOPS, SUCH AS NANTUCKET BAY OR
    TAYLOR BAY (ABOUT 1½ POUNDS)

2 TABLESPOONS UNSALTED BUTTER, AT ROOM TEMPERATURE

HERB SALAD

2 TABLESPOONS CHOPPED FLAT-LEAF PARSLEY

2 TABLESPOONS CHOPPED FRESH TARRAGON

2 TABLESPOONS CHOPPED FRESH CHIVES

2 TABLESPOONS FRESHLY GRATED LEMON ZEST

1 TABLESPOON EXTRA-VIRGIN OLIVE OIL

(continued)

Heat 2 tablespoons of the grapeseed oil in a large skillet over medium heat. When it's hot, add the onion and cook for about 3 minutes, or until softened and lightly browned. Add the squash and chestnuts, cover, and cook for 4 to 6 minutes, stirring occasionally, or until the squash softens a little.

Add the cooked grains, stock, cider, and apple. Increase the heat to medium-high and simmer until the grains begin to absorb the liquid and become tender.

Stir in the crème fraîche. Season to taste with salt and pepper. Set aside and keep warm.

Heat the remaining 2 tablespoons of grapeseed oil in a large, heavy-bottomed skillet over medium-high heat. Add the scallops. Cook in the hot oil for 2 minutes without moving them, or until they begin to turn opaque. Stir them lightly, add the butter, and cook for 1 to 2 minutes longer, or until the butter melts and the scallops are plump, not split, and are cooked through. Transfer to a warm plate lined with a clean kitchen towel to drain.

To make the herb salad: Mix together the parsley, tarragon, chives, and lemon zest in a small bowl. Toss with the olive oil and season to taste with salt and pepper.

Gently stir about three-quarters of the scallops and three-quarters of the herb salad into the grains. Season to taste with salt and pepper. Divide evenly among 4 warmed bowls. Top with the remaining scallops and herb salad.

AFTER MANY YEARS OF ENVIRONMENTALLY DAMAGING HARVESTING PRACTICES, A LOT OF FISHERMEN ALONG THE NORTHEASTERN SEABOARD HAVE BEGUN TO RAKE THE SCALLOPS TO HARVEST THEM. THEIR HAULS MAY BE SMALLER, BUT THE METHOD PRESERVES THE BEDS SO THAT THE SCALLOPS ARE PLENTIFUL YEAR AFTER YEAR— AND THIS BENEFITS MORE THAN JUST SCALLOP FISHERMEN AND SCALLOP LOVERS: THE BIVALVES AERATE AND FILTER THE SEAWATER, WHICH IS CRUCIAL TO KEEPING THE WATER CLEAN. OFF THE ISLAND OF NANTUCKET, THE SCALLOP INDUSTRY IS COMPLETELY SUSTAINABLE, WHICH IS WHY I LIKE TO USE NANTUCKET SCALLOPS WHENEVER POSSIBLE. EATEN RAW, THEIR FLAVOR IS REMINISCENT OF APPLES, MAKING THEM PERFECT PARTNERS FOR APPLES AND APPLE CIDER.

"USE A SPOON" CHOPPED SALAD

When Paul and I agreed to open Dressing Room, one of his first requests was that there always be a really good chopped salad on the menu. He loved an array of flavors and textures in each bite, and he could go on at length about what a pain it was to eat any salad that was not chopped!

In the spring we rely on raw peapods and asparagus, roasted nuts for crunch, and some kind of fruit such as strawberries and blueberries for the salad. We move to peaches in the summer and apples in the fall, looking for sweetness from both, and include some kind of great local cheese.

Serves 6

1½ CUPS RIESLING VINEGAR OR OTHER WHITE WINE VINEGAR

3 CELERY RIBS, CUT INTO ¼" DICE

2 CARROTS, PEELED AND CUT INTO ¼" DICE

1 LARGE RED BELL PEPPER, SEEDED, AND CUT INTO ¼" DICE

1 HEIRLOOM APPLE, SUCH AS COX'S ORANGE PIPPIN OR ROXBURY RUSSET, PEELED, CORED, AND CUT INTO ¼" DICE

½ LARGE CUCUMBER, PEELED, SEEDED, AND CUT INTO ¼" DICE

1 CUP SLICED TREVISO OR RADICCHIO

1 CUP SLICED ARUGULA

1 CUP THINLY SLICED NAPA, SAVOY, OR OTHER SOFT CABBAGE

3 TABLESPOONS EXTRA-VIRGIN OLIVE OIL

SEA SALT AND FRESHLY GROUND BLACK PEPPER

1½ CUPS CRUMBLED LOCAL GOAT CHEESE

½ CUP TOASTED ALMOND SLIVERS

Bring the vinegar to a simmer in a saucepan over medium heat. Add the celery and carrots. Remove the pan from the heat. Set aside to cool.

When the vinegar is cool, add the bell peppers. Cover and refrigerate until cold.

Strain the chilled vegetables through a sieve. Reserve the vinegar and the vegetables separately.

Mix together the apple, cucumber, treviso, arugula, and cabbage in a large bowl. Add ¼ cup of the reserved vinegar and the oil and toss well. Season to taste with salt and pepper. Add the goat cheese and almonds to the bowl and toss to mix. Divide among 6 small bowls or plates.

HEIRLOOM BEET SALAD
with SAVORY MARSHMALLOWS

Americans love marshmallows whether on the end of a stick roasting over a campfire or submerged in a steaming cup of hot cocoa, but we rarely consider them for savory dishes. Beets and walnuts are naturally sweet and pair beautifully with marshmallows, and all three are delightfully offset by the slightly piquant dressing.

Serves 6

1 QUART WATER

1½ CUPS HIGH-QUALITY RED WINE VINEGAR

½ CUP AGAVE NECTAR

3–4 BABY GOLDEN BEETS

3–4 BABY CHIOGGIA (CANDY CANE) BEETS

3–4 BABY RED BEETS

2 TABLESPOONS RIESLING VINEGAR OR OTHER WHITE WINE VINEGAR

2 TABLESPOONS EXTRA-VIRGIN OLIVE OIL

1 TEASPOON WALNUT OIL

½ TEASPOON SEA SALT

FRESHLY GROUND BLACK PEPPER

¼ CUP FLAT-LEAF PARSLEY

6 SAVORY MARSHMALLOW SQUARES (PAGE 88)

2 CUPS ROASTED WALNUT HALVES (PAGE 89)

Mix together the water, red wine vinegar, and agave nectar in a saucepan. Bring to a simmer over medium heat.

Add the unpeeled golden beets. Cook for 10 to 20 minutes, or until just tender when pierced with a sharp paring knife. Lift from the saucepan with a slotted spoon. Set aside to cool. Repeat with the Chioggia beets and then the red beets. Cooking the beets in this order will keep each from coloring the other. Also, not all varieties of beets cook at the same rate of speed as others. Slip the skins off the beets and put them in separate dishes or bowls so that the beets don't bleed into each other. Discard the poaching liquid.

Stir together the vinegar, olive oil, and walnut oil in a small bowl. Season with the salt and pepper.

(continued)

Mix the parsley with two-thirds of the walnuts in a large mixing bowl. Drizzle with two-thirds of the dressing and toss well. Drizzle the remaining dressing over the peeled beets, making sure they are well coated.

Arrange the salad next to a marshmallow on each of 6 plates. Intermittently poke some of each type of beet into the salads to ensure a nice balance of colors. (You could also toss the beets with the other vegetables to make serving easier, although they are apt to bleed into the salad.) Garnish with the remaining walnuts.

SAVORY MARSHMALLOWS

Marshmallows are surprisingly easy to make, although working with the hot syrup demands great care, and you might want the kids to stand clear when you are pouring and beating it. My recipe makes more than you will need for the salad, but it's not easy to make less. And I doubt you will have any trouble getting rid of the leftovers!

Makes one 9" batch

3 ENVELOPES UNFLAVORED KNOX GELATIN

2 CUPS ORGANIC GRANULATED SUGAR

$2/3$ CUP WARM AGAVE NECTAR

1 GOOD-SIZE, STURDY SPRIG FRESH THYME OR ROSEMARY

A FEW LIGHTLY SMASHED BASIL STEMS (ABOUT $1/4$ OUNCE)

$3/4$ TEASPOON KOSHER SALT

1 TEASPOON PURE VANILLA EXTRACT

Lightly oil 2 sheets of parchment, each large enough to line the bottom of a 9" × 9" brownie pan. Slide 1 piece of parchment into the pan and oil the sides of the pan. Set the other sheet aside.

Sprinkle the gelatin over $1/2$ cup cold water in the bowl of an electric mixer fitted with the whisk attachment. Let it soak for about 10 minutes, or until fully softened.

Mix together the sugar, agave nectar, thyme sprig, and smashed basil stems in a small saucepan. Add $1/4$ cup of water, bring to a rapid boil over medium-high heat, and boil for about 1 minute. Pour the boiling syrup through a strainer into a heat-safe container. Use great care.

Pour the hot syrup into the gelatin, add the salt, and beat at high speed for 10 to 12 minutes, or until the mixture is smooth and resembles Marshmallow Fluff. Add the vanilla extract and mix well.

Using an oiled rubber spatula and working quickly, scrape the marshmallow into the prepared pan in a single batch. (This way you avoid mixing oil through the marshmallow mixture.) Set the other piece of oiled parchment, oiled side down, on top of the marshmallow and press gently to distribute the marshmallow evenly in the pan. Remove the top piece of parchment. Let the mixture cool slightly, and then score it into squares or rectangles.

Let the mixture sit for at least 4 hours or overnight. With a thin, lightly oiled knife, cut the marshmallow into the desired shapes.

ROASTED WALNUT HALVES

Makes about 2 cups

- ½ CUP AGAVE NECTAR
- ¼ CUP MOLASSES
- ¼ CUP ORGANIC GRANULATED SUGAR
- 2 TEASPOONS SEA SALT
- ½ TEASPOON FRESHLY GROUND BLACK PEPPER
- 2 CUPS WALNUT HALVES (ABOUT 6½ OUNCES)

Preheat the oven to 400°F.

Bring the agave nectar, molasses, sugar, salt, and pepper to a boil in a small saucepan over medium heat.

Add the walnuts. Return to a strong simmer, and cook for about 6 minutes.

Set a rack on a baking sheet. Pour the mixture over the rack so that the liquid drains to the pan. Push the walnuts away from each other so that they do not stick together.

Transfer the rack holding the walnuts to a clean baking sheet and bake for 5 to 6 minutes, or until the nuts are browned and crispy. Watch the nuts carefully so that they don't scorch. Cool to room temperature before storing.

WATERMELON
and ARUGULA SALAD

Cooks and wine lovers often apply the rule of "marriage of similarity" when selecting wines to go with foods, and yet anyone who has experienced Spätlese with mushrooms or Sauternes with liver mousse knows that pairing opposites can be exciting too. This phenomenon is called marriage of opposites attract.

Here, we apply fruit to vegetable. I cannot take credit for this amazing combination, as I have seen it in a number of restaurants in several countries. It is most popular in Italian-inspired kitchens, and my guess is that the pairing first happened where arugula is native, in Portugal and Morocco and as far as Jordan.

Watermelon, like all melons, is indigenous to tropical America, so I believe this salad or something similar evolved in Italian hands. A good balsamic vinegar strengthens the notion that this dish is nothing new and that Italian-American cooks recognized how the two complement each other. I see it as a great cross-cultural marriage of opposites, as well as a culinary one. Whatever the heck it is, it's delicious.

Serves 4 to 6

- I SMALL WATERMELON (ABOUT 4–4½ POUNDS)
- I CUP WHITE BALSAMIC VINEGAR
- I SMALL SPRIG ROSEMARY
- FRESH LEMON JUICE
- ¼–½ CUP EXTRA-VIRGIN OLIVE OIL
- SEA SALT AND FRESHLY GROUND BLACK PEPPER
- 4 CUPS LOOSELY PACKED ARUGULA (ABOUT 2 OUNCES)
- ½ CUP SHEEP'S MILK FETA CHEESE (AVAILABLE AT MANY FARMERS' MARKETS AROUND THE COUNTRY)
- ½ CUP PITTED WHOLE GREEN OR BLACK OLIVES, CHOPPED
- ½ CUP SHELLED, ROASTED PISTACHIOS, HALVED OR BROKEN INTO LARGE PIECES

Cut the watermelon in half through the equator (consider the place where the stem meets the melon as the North Pole). Turn each melon half cut side down. Slice the rind off starting at the pole and moving down to the cutting board in smooth knife strokes. Cut each melon lobe in half from the pole down. You will notice the seed pattern. Eyeball it as best you can and cut large pieces of the melon meat that has no seeds away from the part that has seeds. Reserve the seedy part and cut each of the seedless pieces into large squares or rectangles that are at least 1" to 1½" thick. Set aside.

Now set a colander inside a large, nonreactive bowl. Get your kids to place the seedy melon flesh in the colander and smash away! The goal is to get as much juice as possible without forcing too much melon flesh through the colander. Strain the juice through a fine-mesh sieve.

Combine the melon juice (not to exceed 2 cups, although you probably will have more than that), vinegar, and rosemary in a small, stainless steel saucepan and bring to a simmer over medium heat. Skim off any foam that rises to the surface. Once fully skimmed and clean, remove the rosemary stem (it will get too strong if you leave it in). Reduce the heat to low and simmer for about 30 minutes, or until reduced to $1/2$ cup.

Transfer the reduced juice to a glass, ceramic, or other nonreactive bowl and set aside to cool. When cool, taste the reduction. If it is very sweet, add lemon juice until it is tangy. If it needs more rosemary, return the stem to the liquid. Whisk in the oil. Season to taste with salt and pepper.

Toss the arugula and feta cheese with enough dressing to coat the leaves lightly. Season with salt and pepper.

Lightly season each melon cube with pepper and arrange the melon cubes on chilled salad plates, leaving space between the cubes for the greens. Add the greens. Sprinkle with the olives and pistachios. Drizzle each plate decoratively with more of the dressing.

ARTISAN CHEESES

GOOD CHEESE STARTS WITH GOOD MILK. THE BEST MILK COMES FROM HAPPY COWS, SHEEP, AND GOATS THAT FEED ON GRASSES GROWING IN LARGE PASTURES WHERE THE ANIMALS CAN ROAM AND CHOMP ON WHATEVER POPS OUT OF THE GROUND. THIS IS THE FIRST STEP IN THE PROCESS FOR MAKING GREAT CHEESE. THE NEXT IS TO COMBINE THE BEST OF OLD-WORLD TECHNIQUES WITH MODERN SCIENCE. GOOD ARTISANAL-CHEESE MAKERS UNDERSTAND THIS, AND THE BEST CRAFT THE TASTIEST CHEESES AVAILABLE.

AT DRESSING ROOM, WE BUY CHEESE FROM BEAVER BROOK FARM IN LYME, CONNECTICUT; BELTANE FARM IN LEBANON, CONNECTICUT; AND CATO CORNER FARM IN COLCHESTER, CONNECTICUT. ALL ARE TERRIFIC PLACES FOR LOCAL, ARTISANAL CHEESES. SEARCH YOUR OWN REGION FOR FARMS WHERE CHEESE IS MADE OR WHERE THE MILK IS SOLD TO SMALL CHEESE MAKERS IN THE AREA. YOU WILL BE REWARDED WITH AMAZING PRODUCTS.

CANDIED QUINCE, PEAR,
and GOAT CHEESE TART

Quinces are indigenous to North America, remarkably beautiful, fragrant, and delicious. And yet quinces are in decline, and I have heard ethnobotanists declare them endangered. I can't urge you more strongly to seek quinces out at farmers' markets. This fruit, which resembles a misshapen apple, has a floral scent with undertones of hard spices such as cardamom, mace, and coriander. Depending on how you cook them, they can be savory or sweet. I love them pureed and served under roasted chicken for a savory dish, although they also turn up in sweet tarts and pies. But this tart is simply a magnificent use of quince, which is astonishing when paired with cheese. The pears needed here should be what I call semiripe, which means they feel just a little softer than an apple. If they are too soft, they will collapse during cooking.

Serves 8

1 (2-POUND) SOURDOUGH BOULE OR SIMILAR ROUND LOAF

2 TABLESPOONS EXTRA-VIRGIN OLIVE OIL

COARSE SEA SALT

1½ CUPS CRUMBLED YOUNG GOAT CHEESE

2 TABLESPOONS FRESH THYME

2 TABLESPOONS GRATED LEMON ZEST

2 CUPS CANDIED QUINCE (OPPOSITE PAGE)

2 SEMIRIPE PEARS

Preheat the oven to 400°F.

Slice the bottom crust from the boule with a long serrated knife. Discard the bottom crust or save it for another use. Cut a 1"-thick slice off the bottom of the loaf. Brush both sides with the oil until it is absorbed. Set aside the rest of the loaf for another use.

Heat a large, heavy-bottomed skillet over medium heat. Cook the oiled bread for about 2 minutes on each side, or until nicely browned. Transfer to a baking sheet and sprinkle lightly with salt.

Toss together the cheese, thyme, and lemon zest in a small bowl. Spread about two-thirds of the quince over the bread slice. Top with about a third of the cheese mixture.

Peel, core, and slice the pears. Arrange about two-thirds of them over the cheese. Top with another third of the cheese mixture. Arrange the remaining quince and pears on top of the cheese in a decorative pattern. Top with the remaining cheese.

Transfer to the oven and bake for 12 to 15 minutes, or until the cheese is lightly browned and the tart is heated through. Cut into wedges and serve.

CANDIED QUINCE

You can double the recipe to make twice the amount of candied quince. It's terrific served with any kind of cheese or spread on crackers.

Makes about 2 cups

I LARGE QUINCE (ABOUT ¾ POUND)

I CUP WATER

½ CUP DRY RIESLING WINE

½ CUP SUGAR

½ CUP LIGHT BROWN SUGAR

I CINNAMON STICK

2 TEASPOONS FRESH LEMON JUICE

Peel the quince and quarter it lengthwise. Slice the core off of each quarter and discard. Cut each wedge crosswise into thin slices.

Mix together the sliced quince with the water, wine, sugars, and cinnamon stick in a saucepan. Bring to a boil over high heat. Reduce the heat so that the mixture simmers gently.

Cook over low heat for 1½ to 2 hours, or until the quince is tender. Adjust the heat up or down to maintain a very low simmer. When the quince is done, the liquid should be the consistency of warm honey. If not, drain the quince and return the syrup to the pan to reduce a little more. Stir in the lemon juice. Discard the cinnamon stick.

Cool to room temperature and use or refrigerate in a tightly lidded container for up to 2 weeks.

CHICKEN LIVER MOUSSE

If I had a nickel for every time I have seen someone throw away a chicken liver, I could afford a private island! (Well . . . maybe a used car.) Considering the nutritional benefits of livers, not to mention their rich flavor, it's a real shame they end up in the trash. I like to share methods and recipes for preparing them, from stewing, frying, and baking to adding them to stuffings. This encourages people to "save the liver," as the ever-ebullient Julia Child often said.

Here is one of my perennial favorites. I call it chicken liver mousse, but it's also known as chopped liver, liver pâté, or liver spread. Whatever you call it, it's outstanding and one of the best ways to get people to try chicken liver. Nearly everyone loves its smooth, buttery texture and opulent flavor, both of which are amazing when served with something crisp. The mousse also complements a variety of other foods, such as fruits, spices, and mushrooms.

Serves 6 to 8

MOUSSE

3 tablespoons unsalted butter

¼ cup peeled, cored, and chopped tart apple

2–3 shallots, thinly sliced

½ teaspoon freshly grated lemon zest

8 ounces raw chicken livers, well trimmed,
   at room temperature

3 tablespoons brandy

1 tablespoon fresh thyme

1 teaspoon fresh tarragon

½ cup + 2 tablespoons heavy cream

Kosher salt and freshly ground black pepper

TOASTS

1 baguette or other long loaf of your choosing,
   such as cranberry-walnut, semolina, or whole wheat

Extra-virgin olive oil

2–3 tablespoons fresh thyme

Kosher salt and freshly ground black pepper

(continued)

To make the mousse: Melt 2 tablespoons of the butter in a large skillet over medium heat. Add the apple, shallots, and lemon zest. Cook, covered, for about 4 minutes, or until the apple and shallots soften.

Increase the heat to high. Add the livers, brandy, thyme, and tarragon. Stir for 2 to 3 minutes, or until the livers just begin to get firm. Cook for about 10 minutes. Transfer to the bowl of a food processor fitted with the metal blade. Add the remaining 1 tablespoon of softened butter and process until smooth. Force the liver through a fine-mesh sieve into a glass mixing bowl.

Meanwhile, whip the cream until soft peaks form in the clean bowl of an electric mixer fitted with the whisk attachment set on medium-high speed. Season with salt and pepper. Raise the speed to high and beat until the peaks are almost firm but not stiff.

Fold the whipped cream into the livers until well incorporated. Cover and refrigerate for at least 30 minutes before serving.

To make the toasts: Heat a heavy skillet over medium heat.

Slice the bread on the bias into ½"-thick slices. Brush each slice well with oil. Brown the slices in the skillet until crisp on both sides. While still warm, sprinkle the warmest side with the thyme and season to taste with salt and pepper. Put in a warm place to hold. Alternatively, crisp the bread in a 375°F oven to save space on the stove top.

To serve, spread a little pâté over the toasts. Sprinkle with fresh thyme. Arrange the toasts on a platter.

ONION-THYME FLATBREAD

A common food memory for folks my age and older is the smell of fresh bread filling the house and half the neighborhood. Not only did it serve as a powerful appetizer for us kids coming home from school, it also attracted half the neighborhood kids and even some of the grown-ups! Bread is one of the simplest and most inexpensive food staples of all time. It's truly miraculous that ingredients as simple as flour, water, salt, and yeast can produce such amazing aromas and be so satisfying to our hunger.

While this is a yeast bread, it requires very little work or skill to make, and the end result is terrific. If we were in Italy, we would call this focaccia. The dough has to rise only once for about 45 minutes before it's baked for less than half an hour. I love this bread alongside simple salads, with a glass of wine or just as is. My wife, Lori, loves it because it makes the house smell like she's been slaving all day. The onion-thyme topping is intentionally scant, but it adds just enough flavor. If you double or triple it, the bread becomes more of an "onion pizza"— which is fine too! The leftovers make great salad croutons.

Makes 2 loaves; serves 8 to 10

BREAD

3 CUPS LUKEWARM WATER

1 TABLESPOON ACTIVE DRY YEAST

6 CUPS UNBLEACHED ALL-PURPOSE FLOUR

1 TABLESPOON SALT

TOPPING

2 TABLESPOONS OLIVE OIL

1 CUP CHOPPED ONION

1 LARGE GARLIC CLOVE, MINCED

2 TABLESPOONS FRESH THYME

COARSE SEA SALT

To make the bread: Put the water in a large bowl. Sprinkle the yeast over the water and stir until dissolved. Add 3 cups of the flour and mix with a wooden spoon until smooth.

Add the remaining flour and the salt. Stir with the spoon or your hands until well mixed and the dough pulls away from the sides of the bowl. The dough will be tacky. Add up to an additional $\frac{1}{2}$ cup of flour, if necessary, if the dough is too wet.

Cover the bowl with a clean kitchen towel. Set aside in a warm place for about 45 minutes, or until doubled in volume. This dough does not resemble other yeast doughs, as it has not been kneaded until smooth.

Meanwhile, make the topping: Heat 1 tablespoon of the oil in a small skillet over medium heat. When hot, add the onion and garlic. Cook, stirring, for 3 to 4 minutes, or until the onion softens. Stir in the thyme and set aside.

Preheat the oven to 500°F. Lightly oil 2 baking sheets.

Turn out the dough onto a lightly floured surface. Knead lightly 5 or 6 times. Divide the dough in half. Put each half in the center of a baking sheet. Using your fingers, stretch each half of the dough over the sheets into ovals or rounds, each about $\frac{1}{4}$" to $\frac{1}{2}$" thick. These should be rustic and somewhat misshapen. As you work, make small indentations with your finger for a dimpled loaf.

Brush each loaf with the remaining 1 tablespoon of oil. Scatter half of the onion over each loaf. The onion will not cover the loaves but will flavor the bread.

Put the pans in the oven and immediately reduce the heat to 450°F. Bake for 15 to 20 minutes, or until the loaves are golden brown, with slightly darker edges around the indentations. Cool on racks. Tear into pieces or cut into wedges for serving.

GREENS FROM WOODBRIDGE

WOODBRIDGE IS A SMALL TOWN IN CONNECTICUT, A LITTLE NORTHEAST OF WEST-PORT. MORE IMPORTANT, IT IS THE SITE OF OUR FAVORITE FARM FOR GREENS. PERRY HACK, AN ART DIRECTOR TURNED FARMER, USES HIS SENSE OF MARKETING, VARIETY, AND BEAUTY TO SUPPLY AND INSPIRE THE SALAD GREENS. PERRY GROWS AN ARRAY OF CERTIFIED ORGANIC LETTUCE IN GREENHOUSES SO THAT EVEN IN THE WINTER, WE HAVE ACCESS TO LOCAL FRESH GREENS.

WINTER HARVESTING OF GREENS IS NOT UNUSUAL IN MANY REGIONS OF THE COUNTRY, WHICH MEANS YOU MAY BE ABLE TO GET FRESH, LOCAL GREENS AT FARM-ERS' MARKETS MUCH OF THE YEAR. INCREASINGLY, FARMERS' MARKETS ARE STAYING OPEN THROUGH THE WINTER, WHICH IS A BOON FOR FARMERS *AND* FOR US!

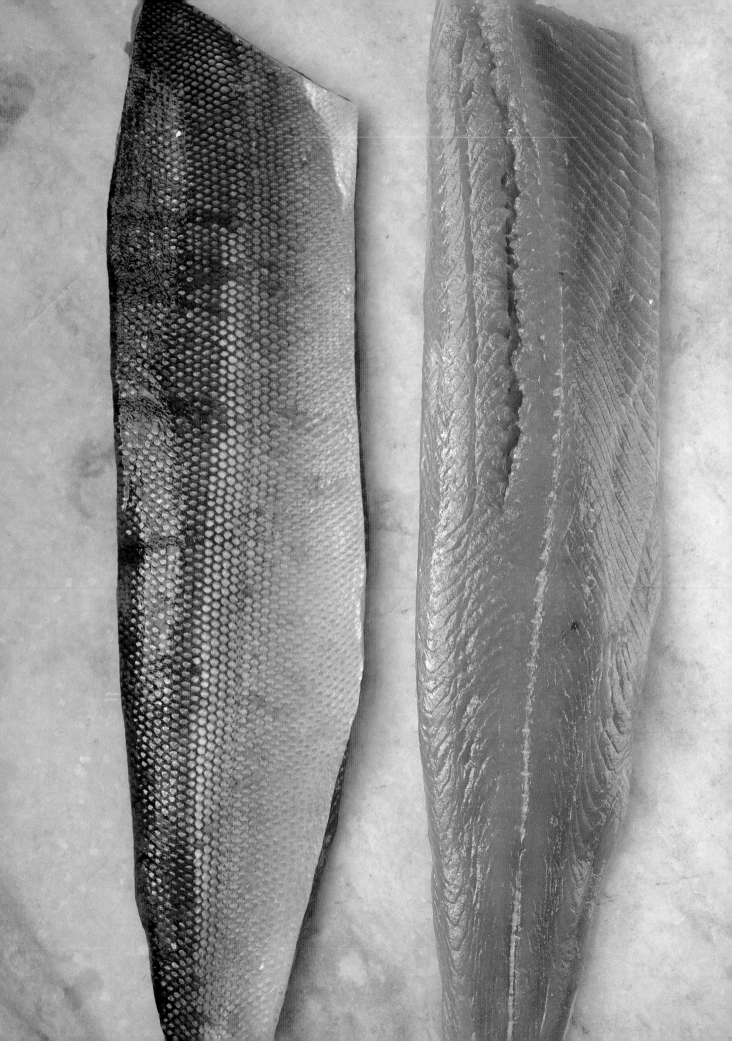

Chapter 4

FISH *and* SEAFOOD

Cooks love fish and seafood—there is hardly a living chef who does not dream up dish after dish that relies on fish. I am no different. The light, fresh flavor of many fish and the succulent richness of shellfish lend themselves to compatible, happy marriages with a host of other ingredients, from greens, grains, and spices to vegetables such as celery root and tomatoes. What's more, fish is bursting with nutrients that feed our bodies even as the flavors feed our soul.

If I could, I would eat fish every day and feed it to my family just as often. Unfortunately, this is not good practice, as our seas are suffering from overfishing and stocks of fish are decreasing. It is our responsibility as stewards of our earth to know which fish are sustainable and therefore acceptable to cook with—and which are not.

Thanks to the help of visionary chefs such as Rick Moonen, Peter Hoffman, Rick Bayless, and others, the Monterey Bay Aquarium, Blue Oceans Institute, and similar organizations have formed to educate the public about the alarmingly waning health of our oceans and fish stocks. Funded by foundations such as the David and Lucile Packard Foundation, chefs, scientists, and environmentalists have formed a broad community of diverse yet like-minded global citizens who encourage consumers to make informed decisions when making seafood choices. The benefits are multiple. Consumers can improve their own well-being while benefiting both the health of the oceans and family-oriented fishing communities.

On these pages, I offer recipes for sustainable fish and seafood. Some, like catfish, are raised in freshwater ponds with little impact on the environment, while others, such as wild-caught salmon, are carefully monitored. I don't advocate eating farmed Atlantic salmon; the salmon are raised in large, densely stocked net pens that pollute surrounding waters with waste and chemicals. Plus, it's not uncommon for the fish to escape, compete for resources, and, even more distressing, breed with or spread parasites to wild fish. On the other hand, it's far better for the environment when we eat farm-raised shrimp than the shrimp harvested by huge trawlers.

When it comes to finfish and seafood, it's tough to keep up with what's safe and responsible to eat. The recipes I offer all pass the test. For more information, go to www.edf.org/home.cfm, the Web site for the Environmental Defense Fund, or www.montereybayaquarium.org, the site for the Monterey Bay Aquarium.

BUTTER-ROASTED OYSTERS

MUSSELS WITH LEEKS AND PINE

TAYLOR BAY SCALLOP LOLLIPOPS

LOBSTER AND SWEET CORN SUCCOTASH

ANGRY CRABS!

NEW FROGMORE STEW

SHRIMP AND GRITS

CREAMED LOUISIANA WHITE SHRIMP
WITH PEPPER-BROWN RICE

PAN-ROASTED BLACKFISH WITH CELERY ROOT PUREE

BUTTER-AND-OIL-POACHED PACIFIC HALIBUT

SEARED WILD SALMON WITH WILTED GREENS
AND ANCIENT GRAINS

SEARED TROUT WITH APPLE-ROSEMARY PUREE

LINE-CAUGHT CHATHAM COD CAKES

SOFT-SHELL CRAB SANDWICH

LINE-CAUGHT CHATHAM COD CAKE SANDWICH

CORNMEAL CATFISH

ALBACORE TUNA MELT

SEARED WILD STRIPED BASS
WITH TOMATO SAGE "FONDUE"

BUTTER-ROASTED OYSTERS

When Paul and I first talked about opening Dressing Room, he asked about the ethics of including a recipe from another restaurant on our menu. I told him it depended on the chef and the restaurant, and when he said he was thinking about the roasted oysters served at Beacon in New York City, I approached my friend and Beacon chef, Waldy Malouf. Waldy is as generous and caring as Paul was, and when I told him Paul wanted the oysters on our menu, he immediately agreed and showed me how he prepared them. I changed the recipe a little, but it's still a simple and beautiful one that celebrates the freshness of the oysters accented primarily by butter and thyme.

Chef Malouf's willingness to share the recipe with me is a nod to the sustainability of friendship and sharing. If we all shared our favorite recipes with each other, everyone would cook more and know more about food. And that would make me happy: Chefs are always happiest in communities where their customers are good cooks!

Serves 4 to 6

⅓ CUP WHITE WINE

¼ CUP GOOD-QUALITY WHITE WINE VINEGAR

1 SHALLOT, THINLY SLICED + 24 THIN SHALLOT SLICES
(ABOUT 4 SHALLOTS)

¼ TEASPOON WHOLE BLACK PEPPERCORNS

½ BAY LEAF

½ CUP (1 STICK) UNSALTED BUTTER, CUT INTO SMALL PIECES

SALT AND FRESHLY GROUND BLACK PEPPER

3–4 CUPS ROCK SALT

2 DOZEN RAW OYSTERS, SHUCKED AND LEFT ON THE HALF SHELL

1 TABLESPOON CHOPPED FRESH THYME

Position the broiler rack as close as possible to the source of the heat. Preheat the broiler.

Heat the wine, vinegar, sliced shallot, peppercorns, and bay leaf in a small saucepan over medium-high heat to a full simmer. Reduce the heat. Cook for 8 to 10 minutes, or until most of the liquid has evaporated and what is left is the consistency of maple syrup.

With the heat on low, whisk in the butter, a few pieces at a time, until all is incorporated. Do not add another piece of butter until the previous one is incorporated. Do not raise the heat. The sauce could break if it gets too hot.

Strain the sauce through a fine-mesh sieve. Season to taste with salt and pepper. Set aside, covered, to keep warm.

(continued)

Spread the rock salt in a single layer in a shallow baking pan that can fit under the broiler, such as a jelly roll pan. The salt will help the oysters stay level when you broil them.

Arrange the oysters, still in their bottom shells, on the salt, making sure they remain as level as possible.

Set a shallot slice over the top of each oyster. Spoon the butter sauce over each oyster.

Broil the oysters for about 5 minutes, or until the sauce browns and breaks slightly. Remove the oysters from the broiler. Sprinkle with the thyme. Season with salt and pepper. Serve warm.

LOCAL OYSTERS

THE OYSTERS I SERVE AT DRESSING ROOM COME FROM WESTPORT'S OWN JEFF NORTHROP. JEFF'S FAMILY HAS OYSTERED THE WATERS OFF OUR BEACHES FOR GENERATIONS, AND WE REAP THE BENEFITS OF HIS KNOWLEDGE AND GREAT CARE. HE KNOWS WHERE THE BEST BEDS ARE AT ANY GIVEN TIME DURING THE SEASON, AND HE NEVER OVERFISHES.

OF COURSE, THE OYSTER BEDS ARE AFFECTED BY RAIN AND OTHER STORMS, AS WELL AS TEMPORARY CLOSINGS OF THE FISHERIES FROM TIME TO TIME. THIS MEANS THAT OCCASIONALLY THE OYSTERS ARE UNAVAILABLE—AND YET, IF YOU'VE TRIED THESE BABIES, YOU KNOW THEY'RE WELL WORTH THE WAIT.

THE FRESHLY HARVESTED OYSTERS COME TO US DIRECTLY FROM JEFF'S BOAT, WHICH MEANS THEY TASTE EVEN BETTER THAN OTHER "FRESH" OYSTERS, WHICH MAY BE STORED FOR UP TO 5 WEEKS BY EVEN THE MOST SCRUPULOUS PURVEYORS. JEFF ALSO SELLS THE OYSTERS AT WESTPORT'S FARMERS' MARKET WHEN THEY ARE IN SEASON—A TREAT FOR LOCAL HOME COOKS.

MUSSELS *with* LEEKS *and* PINE

I was shooting an episode for Lime.com one April with my good friend Loretta Barrett Oden. Joined by master forager Jesse Katz, another dear friend, we foraged our way from California's Santa Cruz Hills to Scott's Creek Beach. Along the way we found chanterelle mushrooms, Monterey pine needles, and, once at the beach, bushels of amazing mussels and fresh kelp. We had wondered aloud what it must have been like to be an Ohlone Indian before their land was seized by settlers; land with abundant reserves of mushrooms, cattail shoots, abalone, mussels, and those beautiful pine needles.

I plucked a pine needle from the end of a branch head, and syrup showed at the tip. I tasted it and decided to cover the mussels and fresh kelp with the pine. We sliced the mushrooms and scattered them among the pine needles and then splashed in a cupped hand of sea water for some seasoning—as well as a can of beer "foraged" right there on the beach, unopened—and cooked our way to heaven. The experience made a lasting impression that I have translated to this recipe. Be sure to use real pine from a tree that has not been sprayed with any sort of pesticide.

Serves 6 to 8

1 OUNCE KELP (SEE NOTE BELOW)

6 DOZEN FRESH MUSSELS, SCRUBBED WELL (ABOUT 3 POUNDS)

2 TABLESPOONS GRAPESEED OIL

1 FENNEL BULB, TRIMMED AND DICED

1 LARGE LEEK, TRIMMED AND CUT INTO ⅛" SLICES (WHITE AND
    LIGHT-GREEN PARTS ONLY)

5 GARLIC CLOVES, MINCED

1½ CUP DRY WHITE WINE

3 TABLESPOONS UNSALTED BUTTER

1 CUP SLICED FLAT-LEAF PARSLEY

SEA SALT AND FRESHLY GROUND BLACK PEPPER

4 HEADS FRESH, UNTREATED PINE NEEDLES (SEE NOTE
    ON OPPOSITE PAGE)

Note: KELP, USUALLY SOLD DRIED OR AS A "SALT," IS A RICH SOURCE OF MINERALS SUCH AS MAGNESIUM, POTASSIUM, IODINE, AND IRON. IT IS ALSO CALLED KOMBU AND WAKAME, BOTH OF WHICH ARE TYPES OF KELP. THE KIND OF KELP MOST COMMONLY SOLD IN THE UNITED STATES IS BLADDERWRACK SEAWEED. IT'S EASY TO FIND IN NATURAL FOOD STORES AND MANY SUPERMARKETS.

Soak the kelp in cold water in a small bowl for 2 hours.

Cover the mussels with cold water in a large bowl or pot. Soak for 20 to 30 minutes to remove any excess dirt or sand.

Heat the oil in a large, heavy stockpot over medium-low heat. Cook the fennel, leek, and garlic for 3 to 5 minutes, or until softened but not browned. Drain. Add the kelp, wine, butter, and $\frac{1}{2}$ cup of the parsley. Increase the heat to medium and bring to a good simmer. Cook for about 15 minutes, or until the liquid reduces by about half. Season to taste with salt and pepper.

Drain the mussels and add to the pot. Lay the pine heads over the mussels, cover the pot, and cook over medium heat for 10 to 12 minutes, or until the shells open.

Remove and discard the pine. Transfer the mussels and cooking juices to a large serving bowl, sprinkling intermittently with the remaining $\frac{1}{2}$ cup parsley. Use the transfer as an opportunity to identify and discard any unopened shells. Serve immediately.

Note : YOU MAY NOT HAVE THE LUXURY OF GATHERING PRISTINE PINE NEEDLES ALONG CALIFORNIA'S COAST, BUT IF YOU HAVE ACCESS TO PINE NEEDLES IN YOUR BACKYARD OR NEARBY WOODS, GATHER ENOUGH TO COVER THE POT. RINSE THEM WELL IN CLEAR, WARM WATER. IF YOU CANNOT FIND THEM, DON'T LET THAT STOP YOU FROM MAKING THE DISH.

TAYLOR BAY
SCALLOP LOLLIPOPS

On a very cold February day, two of my three sons and I traveled to Buzzard's Bay, Massachu-setts, to film a segment for the PBS show Chefs A' Field: Kids on the Farm, *set on Rod Taylor's scalloping boat. It was 17°F on deck as we broke through the ice and braved 15-knot winds to reach and raise the scallop pods. A pod is a suspension net used to grow and then harvest farmed scallops. Rod and I immediately shucked a few and began eating them right out the shell. Both boys, not to be outdone, decided they would do the same. I was dumbfounded to see Drew, an avowed hater of seafood, pop a raw scallop in his mouth and say, "Hmm . . . it tastes like apples!" and promptly ask for another.*

Frying the scallops and skewering them makes them fun to eat, for kids or adults, as a main course or hors d'oeuvre.

Serves 4

DRESSING

1 TABLESPOON FRESH APPLE CIDER

1 TABLESPOON APPLE CIDER VINEGAR

2 TEASPOONS LOCAL HONEY

2 TEASPOONS GRAINY MUSTARD

¼ CUP GRAPESEED OIL

KOSHER SALT AND FRESHLY GROUND BLACK PEPPER

SCALLOPS

1 SMALL RED BEET, SCRUBBED

1 SMALL YELLOW BEET, SCRUBBED

2 TABLESPOONS OLIVE OIL

SEA SALT

20 BAY SCALLOPS, CLEANED (ABOUT ¾ POUND)

½ CUP SPELT OR ALL-PURPOSE FLOUR

1 LARGE EGG

2 TABLESPOONS WATER

½ CUP PLAIN DRIED BREAD CRUMBS (SEE NOTE ON PAGE 114)

1 QUART GRAPESEED OIL

4 CUPS MIXED SALAD GREENS

(continued)

To make the dressing: Whisk together the cider, vinegar, honey, and mustard in a mixing bowl. When blended, keep whisking and add the grapeseed oil in a steady stream until the dressing emulsifies. Season to taste with salt and pepper. Set aside until needed. The dressing will keep in a tightly lidded jar for up to 2 days in the refrigerator.

To make the scallops: Preheat the oven to 375°F.

Rub the beets with the olive oil and sprinkle with a little salt. Put each beet in a separate pan so that their colors don't bleed into each other. Roast for 35 to 45 minutes, or until the beets are tender when pierced with the tip of a sharp knife.

Let the beets cool. When cool enough to handle, slip the skins off. Cut the beets into $1/2$" to $3/4$" dice.

Reduce the oven temperature to 200°F.

Toss the scallops with the flour until lightly coated in a shallow dish.

Put the egg in a shallow dish and whisk with the water. Put the bread crumbs in another shallow dish. Dip the floured scallops first in the egg wash and then in the bread crumbs to coat.

Meanwhile, pour enough of the grapeseed oil into a heavy pot to fill it about halfway. Heat over medium heat until it registers 350°F, or until a piece of bread dropped in the oil browns quickly. Fry 6 to 8 scallops for 2 to 3 minutes, or until lightly browned. Do not crowd the pan. Lift the scallops from the oil with a slotted spoon and set aside to drain in a shallow dish lined with paper towels. Let the oil regain its heat between frying batches of scallops. Insert a 6" or 8" wooden skewer into each scallop. Keep warm in the oven.

Toss the salad greens and beets in a mixing bowl. Toss with the dressing.

Divide the salad equally between the 4 plates and drizzle the plate with a little extra dressing, if desired. Transfer the scallops in a basket or serving bowl lined with compostable paper towels or napkins.

Note: PLEASE MAKE YOUR OWN BREAD CRUMBS. FOR $1/2$ CUP OF CRUMBS, TOAST A GOOD-SIZE SLICE OF HEARTY, COUNTRY-STYLE BREAD, THEN GRIND IT INTO CRUMBS IN A BLENDER OR SMALL FOOD PROCESSOR. PACKAGED CRUMBS MAY BE MIXED WITH A LITTLE SUGAR, WHICH WILL CAUSE THE SCALLOPS TO BROWN TOO QUICKLY BEFORE THEY HAVE COOKED THROUGH.

LOBSTER *and* SWEET CORN SUCCOTASH

Lobster and corn have had a mutual appreciation society since Atlantic coastal Native Americans used lobster shells to fertilize their maize. I call this succotash, but it's far more elegant than you might expect and is squarely in the main-course category. This is a wonderful special meal for summer. It's rich, opulent, and satisfyingly creamy.

Serves 4

2 (1½-pound) lobsters

Kernels from 6 ears sweet corn (about 2 cups kernels)

1 tablespoon grapeseed oil

2 shallots, sliced

1 carrot, peeled and cut into ¼" dice

1 fennel bulb, cut into ¼" dice

3 cups light cream

½ cup cooked Dried Heirloom Beans (page 8)

2 tablespoons unsalted butter, cut into cubes

2 tablespoons minced fresh herbs, such as thyme, tarragon, chervil, and parsley

Kosher salt and freshly ground black pepper

Half-fill a large stockpot with water and bring to a boil over high heat. Put the lobsters head-first into the boiling water. Cover and cook for about 10 minutes, or until the shells turn bright red and the meat is just cooked through. Drain the lobsters and let cool.

Crack the shells and remove the meat from the claws and bodies. Cut into ½" to 1" pieces. You will have a 2 scant cups of lobster meat. Set aside.

Finely chop half of the corn kernels or pulse them in the bowl of a small food processor. Set aside, keeping any juice they release.

Heat the oil in a stockpot over medium heat. Add the shallots and cook for 1 to 2 minutes, or until they begin to soften. Add the carrot and fennel. Reduce the heat to low and cook for 6 to 8 minutes, or until the vegetables begin to soften nicely. Add the reserved whole corn kernels and cook for another 1 to 2 minutes.

Add the cream and the chopped corn kernels and their liquid. Cook over medium-high heat for about 3 minutes, stirring constantly so as not to boil over, until the cream just begins to thicken. Add the reserved meat and cook until the sauce is thickened nicely and the lobster is just heated through and not tough.

Stir in the beans, butter, and herbs. Stir for 2 to 3 minutes, or until heated through. Season to taste with salt and pepper and serve.

ANGRY CRABS!

This recipe was inspired by a dear friend, Pat Trama, who created a dish he called the Angry Lobster when he was the chef at F.illi Ponte restaurant in New York's Tribeca neighborhood. He heated a pan until it was really hot and then cooked a split and cracked live lobster in the searing pan wok-style, with garlic, red-pepper flakes, and broccoli rabe. Pure genius! The heat of the peppers and the bitterness of the broccoli rabe played off the sweetness of the lobster for one of the most delicious shellfish meals I have ever had.

A while ago, I was eating Dungeness crabs, cracking the crabs with hammers and dipping the meat in melted butter. I noticed that my dining companions were shaking copious amounts of red-pepper flakes on the crabs after dipping them in butter. I quickly flashed back to Pat and his incredible lobster dish. My Angry Crabs were born!

This dish will seem like a lot of work, but you will forever be a hero to anyone who samples these angry crabs. If you can find only already-cooked Dungeness crabs—as generally is the case in the eastern half of the country—just skip the step of cooking them.

Serves 6

THE CRABS

2 FENNEL BULBS, SPLIT IN HALF

2 LEMONS, QUARTERED

1 LARGE LEEK, CLEANED AND COARSELY CHOPPED

1 LARGE ONION, QUARTERED

A GOOD PINCH OF SEA SALT

3 LIVE DUNGENESS CRABS

THE ANGER

¾ POUND BROCCOLI RABE, TOUGH STEMS REMOVED

¼ CUP EXTRA-VIRGIN OLIVE OIL

6 TABLESPOONS UNSALTED BUTTER

4 GARLIC CLOVES, SMASHED WITH THE SIDE OF A LARGE KNIFE (NOT MASHED WITH A FORK)

2 SMALL TO MEDIUM SHALLOTS, THINLY SLICED

1–2 TEASPOONS CRUSHED DRIED RED-PEPPER FLAKES

2 TABLESPOONS FRESH-PICKED THYME

2 TABLESPOONS CHOPPED FLAT-LEAF PARSLEY

2 TABLESPOONS THINLY SLICED FRESH LEMON VERBENA LEAVES
OR 2 THIN LEMON SLICES

1/2 CUP DRY RIESLING OR PINOT GRIS

1/4 CUP FRESH GRAPEFRUIT OR ORANGE JUICE

I TABLESPOON GRATED ORANGE ZEST

To cook the crabs: Fill a 3-gallon stockpot about two-thirds full with water. Add the fennel, lemons, leek, onion, and salt. Bring to a boil over high heat. Add the crabs. When the water returns to a boil, reduce the heat to medium-low. Simmer gently for about 20 minutes, or until the crabs cook through and are bright red.

Lift the cooked crabs from the pot. When cool enough to handle, crack the crab legs, but do not remove them from the bodies. Crack open the crab bodies and remove the gristle and any sand.

To make the "anger": Blanch the broccoli rabe for about 3 minutes, or until bright green, in a deep skillet or saucepan filled with simmering water set over medium-high heat. Immediately plunge the broccoli rabe into a bowl full of ice water. Drain, then chop into bite-size pieces. You will have about 2 cups of broccoli rabe.

Heat a large, deep, nonreactive stockpot large enough for the crabs over medium-high heat. When nearly hot, heat 4 tablespoons of the butter and the oil until the butter melts but has not browned. Add the garlic, shallots, and pepper flakes. Cook for 1 to 2 minutes, or until the garlic and shallots begin to soften.

Add the crabs, tossing constantly, for about 8 minutes, or until the crabs begin to heat through. Add the broccoli rabe and half of the thyme, parsley, and lemon leaves. Continue cooking, tossing the mixture for about 5 minutes, or until heated through. Transfer the crabs to a warm serving platter.

Pour the wine and juice into the pan. Bring to a boil, scraping the bottom of the pan with a wooden spoon to deglaze. Stir in the remaining herbs and the orange zest. Cook for 3 to 4 minutes, or until the reduction resembles thin maple syrup. Swirl in the remaining 2 tablespoons of butter. Drizzle the sauce over the crabs. Serve immediately.

NEW FROGMORE STEW

This recipe is a "barely revised" classic from the Outer Banks and Gullah islands of the coastal Carolinas and Georgia. These days, it's near impossible to find a recipe for Frogmore Stew that uses all fresh ingredients. This is an instance of looking back in order to move forward. I use only fresh vegetables, potatoes, shrimp, and herbs in this stew, as well as some great-tasting andouille or boudin sausage. Andouille is a little spicier than boudin; both are top-notch.

Serves 10 to 12

SEA SALT

6 QUARTS WATER

6 GARLIC CLOVES, CHOPPED

2 LARGE ONIONS

2 TABLESPOONS PAPRIKA

2 TEASPOONS DRIED RED-PEPPER FLAKES

1 BUNCH FRESH OREGANO (ABOUT ¼ OUNCE), COARSELY CHOPPED

1 LARGE YUKON GOLD POTATO, PEELED

1 POUND UNPEELED PURPLE POTATOES, COARSELY CHOPPED

1 POUND UNPEELED FINGERLING POTATOES, COARSELY CHOPPED

2 POUNDS SPICY ANDOUILLE OR BOUDIN SAUSAGE

10 EARS CORN, HUSKED AND CUT INTO 1" SEGMENTS

4 POUNDS LARGE FRESH WHITE SHRIMP, UNPEELED

2 TABLESPOONS UNSALTED BUTTER

1 TABLESPOON CHOPPED FRESH DILL

SALT AND FRESHLY GROUND BLACK PEPPER

Salt a very large pot of water just until it tastes slightly less salty than seawater. Add the garlic, onions, paprika, pepper flakes, and oregano. Bring to a boil over high heat. Add the Yukon gold and purple potatoes. Let the water return to a boil and cook for about 5 minutes. Add the fingerling potatoes. Let the water return to a boil and cook for 10 minutes longer.

Cut the sausage in 1½" pieces and add with the corn to the stew. Cook for 5 minutes, then add the shrimp. Gently stir as it cooks for about 5 minutes, or until the shrimp are just cooked through and pink.

Drain the vegetables, sausage, and shrimp through a colander, reserving about 2 quarts of the cooking liquid. Transfer the cooked ingredients to a serving bowl and keep warm.

Transfer 1 quart of the reserved liquid and the Yukon gold potato to a blender. Puree until smooth. Add the butter and dill. Blend just until smooth. Season to taste with salt and pepper.

Pour the puree over the vegetables, shrimp, and sausage. Toss well and serve. Add some of the reserved drained liquid to make the stew more liquid, as needed.

SHRIMP *and* GRITS

I have a theory that seems constant: When you eat the foods that are most available to you from a sustainable viewpoint—meaning they grow or live in the same region—they taste good together. Think of tomatoes and basil, winter squash and maple syrup, cod and potatoes.

Shrimp is a case in point. Native Americans tossed the shells from shrimp, scallops, lobsters, and other crustaceans on their small fields to fertilize the corn. The shells were ideal amendments to the soil, and the corn demanded very little extra help from the hand of man to flourish. Cooks discovered the sweetness of shellfish and the toasty flavor of corn is a winning marriage, and over the years have developed dishes that speak truth to this assumption. Of course, adding a good measure of andouille sausage makes for a fuller, richer dish.

Serves 6

- 1 cup yellow hominy grits (I like Anson Mills antebellum grits) (see note)
- 18 large shrimp (16/20 count), peeled and deveined
- 3 cups buttermilk
- 2½ cups water
- 2 teaspoons sea salt
- 1 cup whole milk
- Salt and freshly ground black pepper
- ¼ cup grated aged sheep's milk cheese, such as Cypress Grove Midnight Moon, or Pecorino Romano
- 1 tablespoon + 1 pint grapeseed oil
- About 5 ounces andouille sausage, halved lengthwise and cut into ¼"- thick slices
- ½ small to medium yellow onion, cut pole to pole into ¼"-thick slices
- 1 red bell pepper, seeded, membranes removed, and cut into 3"-long strips
- 2 cups canned tomatoes, chopped
- 1½ cups cornmeal
- about ¼ cup sliced fresh cilantro for garnish

Cover the hominy grits with water in a mixing bowl. Stir and let the grits settle for a few minutes. Using a small strainer, skim off the chaff and hulls that rise to the surface. Cover the pan. Let the grits stand for at least 8 hours, or overnight.

(continued)

Combine the shrimp and buttermilk in a large bowl a few hours before you are ready to prepare the dish. Cover and refrigerate for 1 to 2 hours.

Drain the grits and transfer to a stockpot. Add the water and sea salt and bring to a gentle simmer over medium heat. Cover the pot. Cook for about 1 hour, stirring occasionally to prevent sticking. Adjust the heat up or down to maintain a low simmer. When done, the grits will be quite thick.

Stir in the milk and cheese until the grits are creamy. Season to taste with salt and black pepper, if necessary. Cover and set aside to keep warm.

While the grits are cooking, heat a saucepan over medium-low heat. When hot, put 1 tablespoon of the oil and the sausage into the pan. Cook, stirring, for 4 to 5 minutes, or until the sausage is lightly browned on both sides. Transfer the sausage to a warm plate and set aside.

Add the onion to the pan and increase heat to medium. Cook for about 5 minutes, or until softened and lightly browned. Add the bell pepper and cook for 3 minutes longer, or until the slices begin to soften. Stir in the tomatoes, reduce the heat to low, and cook, uncovered, for 15 to 20 minutes, or until the vegetables reach a saucelike consistency. Return the sausage to the pan. Adjust the seasoning with salt and black pepper. Cover and keep warm.

Heat the remaining pint of oil in a deep skillet over medium heat until shimmering hot. The skillet should be large enough so that the oil is at least ¼" deep.

Meanwhile, put the cornmeal in a shallow bowl.

Drain the shrimp, but do not wipe them dry. Sprinkle with salt and black pepper. Toss the shrimp in the cornmeal until well coated.

Fry the shrimp in the hot oil for 5 to 6 minutes, or until golden brown on both sides. Be careful not to overcook. Cook the shrimp in batches if it's easier or if your pan is not large enough for all of them at once. Transfer to a plate lined with a clean kitchen towel to drain. If you fry the shrimp in batches, let the oil regain its heat between batches.

Make sure the grits are nice and hot. If they seem too thick, thin them with warm milk. Spoon the grits into 8 small serving dishes, such as ramekins. Arrange the shrimp and sausage on serving plates or a large platter and serve the sauce on the side.

Note: IF YOU CAN'T FIND HOMINY GRITS, USE ANY OLD-FASHIONED, SLOW-COOKING GRITS AND COOK THEM ACCORDING TO THE PACKAGE DIRECTIONS.

CREAMED LOUISIANA WHITE SHRIMP
with PEPPER-BROWN RICE

I recall one of my uncles liked his biscuits and gravy with shrimp. He had spent time in the Carolinas, Georgia, and north Florida, which I guess is where he picked up this habit. When you first encounter it, the notion of shrimp with milk and bacon gravy sounds, well, gross, but smoked pork, shrimp, and dairy like each other enough to make this dish work—think shrimp and carbonara sauce.

Shrimp cooked this way reminds me of the white gravy and peppery rice my mom cooked when she fried chicken. The combo has a high comfort factor. When you sit down to eat it, it's pretty heavy, so I like to serve three shrimp per person and along with the Pan-Wilted Kale with Pear and Cured Berkshire Pork Belly on page 212 or the Fresh Heirloom Beans on page 217. If you are really hungry and have been eating wisely for the last few days, go for broke and serve 6 shrimp per person.

Warning: There will be no leftovers!

Serves 12 as an appetizer or 6 as an entrée

RICE

2 TEASPOONS GRAPESEED OIL

4–5 SLICES BACON, CUT INTO SMALL, SQUARISH PIECES

½ CUP DICED ONION

1 TEASPOON FRESHLY GROUND BLACK PEPPER

3 CUPS BROWN RICE

4½ CUPS HOT SAVORY VEGETABLE STOCK (PAGE 20) OR HOT WATER

SHRIMP

36 SWEET WHITE SHRIMP, HEADS LEFT ON, BODIES PEELED AND SHELLS RESERVED

3 CUPS HEAVY CREAM

SEA SALT AND FRESHLY GROUND BLACK PEPPER

½ CUP THINLY SLICED SHALLOTS

½ CUP WHITE WINE

2 TABLESPOONS FRESH THYME

2 TABLESPOONS GRATED AGED SHEEP'S MILK OR GOAT CHEESE

To cook the rice: Heat the oil in a skillet over medium heat. When hot, cook the bacon for 2 to 3 minutes, or until crispy. Remove the bacon and drain on paper towels. Reserve the bacon fat.

Heat 2 tablespoons of the bacon fat in a saucepan over medium heat. Add the onion and cook for 5 to 6 minutes, or until softened but not browned. Season with the pepper. Cook for about 1 minute longer.

Add the rice. Cook until the rice feels hot to the touch. Pour the hot stock or water into the pan. Bring to a simmer over medium-high heat. Stir once or twice, reduce the heat to low, cover tightly, and cook for 40 to 45 minutes, or until the liquid is fully absorbed. Do not remove the lid until the rice has been cooking for at least 30 minutes.

Remove the pan from the heat. Let it sit, covered, for 10 minutes. Remove the lid and gently fluff the rice with a fork.

Meanwhile, cook the shrimp: Cook the reserved shrimp shells in a deep stockpot, stirring constantly, until the shells turn bright pinky orange. Add the cream. Bring to a simmer over medium-high heat, reduce the heat to medium-low, and simmer for about 40 minutes, or until reduced by half. Take care that the cream does not boil at any point.

Strain the cream through a fine-mesh sieve, pressing the shells vigorously to squeeze out any remaining cream and flavor. Discard the shells.

Season the shrimp with salt and pepper.

Heat a large, deep skillet over medium heat. When hot, add 2 tablespoons of the reserved bacon fat (discard any remaining). Add the shrimp, shallots, and bacon. Cook for 1 to 2 minutes, or until the shrimp is pink on one side. Turn the shrimp and cook for 1 to 2 minutes longer, or until they are pink on both sides and the shallots are soft. Remove the shrimp with a slotted spoon. Set aside, covered, to keep warm.

Add the wine to the skillet. Cook for about 3 minutes, or until the wine reduces by about half. Return the shrimp to the skillet. Add the reduced cream and the thyme. Simmer for 3 minutes, or until the shrimp finish cooking. Stir in the grated cheese. Serve spooned over the rice.

PAN-ROASTED BLACKFISH
with CELERY ROOT PUREE

The season for the famed tautog fish, also called blackfish, runs from early in the fall through the end of December. If the phrase "you are what you eat" ever applied to a fish, it would apply to the tautog, which gets its firm flesh and rich, lobstery flavor from the lobster and crab that this powerful denizen of the deep munches on. Its flavor is truly amazing and, when paired with Celery Root Puree, evokes the spirit of the early Thanksgivings the settlers shared with the Native Americans when the fish was a staple for all the inhabitants of the original 13 colonies.

Blackfish has been prized in New England for centuries, although it fell out of favor as Americans decided they preferred fish that tasted less like, well, fish! Today, we have thankfully learned enough to buy the richest-tasting meat, the earthiest-tasting vegetables, and the most succulent fruit, so for really good-tasting fish, try blackfish. It is not particularly "fishy" but is packed with flavor and incredibly rich meat. Blackfish fishing is also a sustainable operation, involving smaller boats, often family-owned. Buying it supports sustainable types of fishing methods that will ensure the enjoyment of recipes like this one for generations to come.

Serves 6

6 (6 ounces each) skinless blackfish fillets

Sea salt and freshly ground black pepper

2 tablespoons grapeseed oil

1 pound mushrooms, trimmed and sliced

2 tablespoons diced shallot

1 cup chopped homegrown, canned tomatoes, with enough
   of the liquid to keep the tomatoes juicy

2 tablespoons unsalted butter

2 tablespoons sliced fresh chives

3 celery ribs, trimmed

¼ cup tender celery leaves

2 tablespoons barely chopped flat-leaf parsley

2 teaspoons freshly grated lemon zest

1 tablespoon extra-virgin olive oil

1 teaspoon fresh lemon juice

Celery Root Puree (page 210)

Season the fillets with salt and pepper.

Heat the grapeseed oil in a large, heavy skillet over medium-high heat. When hot, cook the fish, skin side down (or what used to be the skin sides), for 3 to 4 minutes, or until nicely browned.

Turn the fillets over using a thin, flexible spatula. Add the mushrooms and shallot to the pan. Cook for 4 to 5 minutes, carefully stirring the shallot and mushrooms around in the pan without disturbing the fillets, until the mushrooms give off their liquid and the fish is cooked through. You may want to do this is batches or use 2 pans. Transfer the fillets to a warm plate and cover loosely with foil. Keep warm in a 250°F oven.

Cover the pan. Cook the mushrooms and shallot for about 5 minutes longer, or until the mushrooms release all their juices. Remove the lid and let the mushrooms and shallot cook for 3 to 4 minutes longer, or until the pan is dry.

Add the tomatoes and butter. Cook for 2 to 3 minutes, stirring, until the butter emulsifies into a sauce. Season to taste with salt and pepper. Remove the pan from the heat. Stir in the chives. You will have about 2 cups.

Using a vegetable peeler, shave the celery into long, spaghetti-like strands. You will have about 3 cups of loosely packed strands. Put them in a bowl with the celery leaves, parsley, and lemon zest. Sprinkle with the olive oil and lemon juice. Toss well. Season to taste with salt and pepper.

To serve, spoon puree onto each of 6 plates. Rest a fillet against each mound. Spoon some sauce over each one. Top with the celery salad.

BUTTER-AND-OIL-POACHED PACIFIC HALIBUT

Fish poached in butter and oil is truly amazing—you have to taste it to believe it. And yes, although it's cooked in fat, it's not necessarily unhealthy. I have done my research and can assure you that while it's never a good idea to eat fat with abandon, if you mainly eat monoun- saturated and polyunsaturated fats, you will be fine. Even butter now and then is not a bad thing. As the father of two sons who live with diabetes, I am very careful about what I serve them, and this dish, while not an everyday affair, is fine every now and then. I suggest you combine fats with ingredients containing soluble fiber, such as beans, cruciferous vegetables (like broccoli and Brussels sprouts), and whole grains such as farro and barley. In this recipe, the butter and oil are the cooking medium, and I can't deny that they add extra calories. But taste the fish! It's fantastic.

For more on fats and their impact, visit the Harvard School for Public Health's Web site at www.hsph.harvard.edu/nutritionsource.

Serves 4 to 6

SPICE MIXTURE

2 TABLESPOONS GREEN OR OTHER FENNEL SEEDS

2 TEASPOONS SEA SALT

2 TEASPOONS ORGANIC RAW SUGAR

2 TEASPOONS FRESHLY GRATED LEMON ZEST

FRESHLY GROUND BLACK PEPPER

HALIBUT

1 LARGE SKINLESS PACIFIC HALIBUT FILLET (ABOUT 2–3 POUNDS AND NO MORE THAN 2" THICK)

3 CUPS EXTRA-VIRGIN OLIVE OIL

1 CUP (2 STICKS) UNSALTED BUTTER

2–3 CHIOGGIA (CANDY CANE) OR GOLDEN BEETS, PEELED AND CUT INTO ¼"-THICK SLICES

2 FENNEL BULBS, TRIMMED, FRONDS RESERVED, AND FENNEL CUT LENGTHWISE INTO ¼"-THICK SLICES

1½ CUPS WHOLE SMALL RADISHES, CLEANED BUT NOT PEELED

1 POUND GRAPE OR PEAR TOMATOES, PIERCED

8 garlic cloves, smashed

Zest of 1 lemon

12 fresh lemon verbena leaves + more for garnish,
    or 4–6 thin lemon slices

Green fennel seeds, for garnish

To prepare the spice mixture: Lightly mash the fennel seeds, salt, sugar, lemon zest, and pepper to taste in a mortar with a pestle until the fennel seeds are broken and the mixture is fragrant.

To cook the halibut: Rub the spice mixture over the fish. Set the fish aside for about 30 minutes to come to room temperature. Do not let the fish sit out for more than 30 minutes; if you must, refrigerate it so that it does not run the risk of spoiling.

Meanwhile, heat the oil and butter in a skillet, stockpot, or small roasting pan, large enough to hold the fish comfortably, over medium heat until the butter melts. (If necessary, cut the fish in half and reassemble once cooked.) Do not let the fats get too hot. Add the beets, fennel, radishes, tomatoes, garlic, and lemon zest and simmer, stirring occasionally, for about 30 minutes, or until the vegetables are tender but still fully intact.

With a slotted spoon or pasta strainer, transfer the vegetables to a colander to drain. Set aside, covered, to keep warm. Leave the butter and oil in the pan.

Put the fish, lemon verbena, and about half of the fennel fronds in the skillet or roasting pan so they are fully submerged in the oil and butter. If they are not, gently force the remaining fennel fronds in the pan to raise the level of the oil and butter so that the fat covers the fish.

Cover the fish with parchment paper so that it sits directly on top of the butter and oil. Cook just below a simmer for about 5 minutes. Remove from the heat. Let stand, covered, for 10 to 12 minutes, or until the fish finishes cooking in the warm butter and oil.

Gently transfer the fish to a warm serving platter. If necessary, gently tilt the pan while holding the fish in place as you discard some of the oil and butter, which will make the transfer easier. You might need assistance doing this, as the pan will be heavy. Discard the fennel stems and verbena.

Reheat the vegetables in the liquid remaining in the pan over medium heat just until hot. Arrange the vegetables around the fillet. Sprinkle with green fennel seeds and lemon verbena.

SEARED WILD SALMON *with* WILTED GREENS *and* ANCIENT GRAINS

Salmon loves to be served alongside foods that are more fully flavored than itself. Its soft butteriness calls out for a wilted green with character and strength, along with grains that stand up to both. This is where ancient grains are so wonderful. They are tasty and healthful, being a high-fiber carbohydrate whose glucose takes a while to convert to sugar. I think it's important to design meals so that you have a high-quality protein, a high-quality vegetable, and some interesting carbohydrates.

When you can find wild-caught salmon, buy it. Alaska's wild fisheries are well managed, so it's not irresponsible to cook what they send to market. Also, it comes from very cold waters, and for this reason, wild Alaskan salmon freezes well.

Serves 4

1¾ CUPS COOKED BLACK BARLEY (PAGE 10)

1¾ CUPS COOKED FARRO (PAGE 10)

½ CUP COOKED DRIED HEIRLOOM BEANS (PAGE 8)

½ CUP SAVORY VEGETABLE STOCK (PAGE 20) OR HIGH-QUALITY COMMERCIAL STOCK

½ CUP QUARTERED GRAPE TOMATOES

SALT AND FRESHLY GROUND BLACK PEPPER

2 POUNDS WILD-CAUGHT SALMON FILLET WITH SKIN ON

2 TABLESPOONS GRAPESEED OIL

1 TEASPOON THINLY SLICED GARLIC CLOVES

4 CUPS PACKED SPINACH OR OTHER WILTING GREEN, WELL RINSED WITH SOME WATER STILL CLINGING TO THE LEAVES

3-4 FRESH BASIL LEAVES, TORN INTO PIECES

1 TABLESPOON EXTRA-VIRGIN OLIVE OIL

Combine the grains and beans with the stock in a saucepan. Bring to a simmer over medium heat. Cook, uncovered, for 6 to 8 minutes, or until most of the stock evaporates. Stir in the tomatoes. Season to taste with salt and pepper. Set aside, covered, to keep warm.

Season the skin side of the salmon with salt and pepper. Drizzle with almost half of the grapeseed oil.

Heat a large skillet over medium-high heat. When hot, cook the fillets, skin side down, for 2 to 3 minutes, or until the skin is crisp and nicely browned. Season the flesh side of the fillets with salt and pepper. Drizzle with a little more of the oil. Turn the fillets over.

Add the rest of the oil to the pan along with the garlic. Cook for about 1 minute, or until the garlic starts to brown. Remove the fillets from the pan and set aside on a warmed serving platter.

Add the spinach to the pan. Cook over medium heat for 1 to 2 minutes, or until fully wilted. Season the spinach with salt and pepper.

Add the basil to the grains and stir well to mix. Mound the grains on the center of each of 4 warmed plates and divide the spinach among the plates, putting it next to the grains. Lay the salmon fillets over the grains and greens so that both can be seen beneath the salmon. Drizzle each serving with olive oil and serve.

You can serve this family-style by mounding the grains in the center of a platter and placing the spinach around the grains. Top with the salmon fillets and drizzle with olive oil.

SEARED TROUT
with APPLE-ROSEMARY PUREE

When you're looking for something sustainable and delicious, trout is a great choice. At Dressing Room, we buy trout from the Sunburst Trout Company in Canton, North Carolina, where the fish swim in clean mountain water and are fed in a manner that is good for both the fish and the beautiful mountain environment they inhabit.

From a flavor perspective, trout is versatile. I've happily eaten it with brown butter and almonds, lemon and capers, and breaded and baked—as have most of us. As delicious as all these preparations are, the natural nuttiness of the fish's flesh invites an entirely different approach. Some folks might find it odd that we pair trout with apples and rosemary, but trust me when I say the combination is out of this world! As rule, I am not a fan of fruit with fish, but the rosemary creates a flavor bridge that makes this combination simply perfect.

Serves 4

APPLE-ROSEMARY PUREE

2½ pounds tart heirloom apples (about 6 apples), such as Cox's Orange Pippin, Newtown Pippin, Roxbury Russet, or real Granny Smiths, peeled, cored, and sliced

2 cups water

1 cup apple juice

1 cup heavy cream

1 large rosemary sprig

4 tablespoons unsalted butter, softened

¼–½ teaspoon fine sea salt

Freshly ground black pepper

TROUT

8 trout fillets, halved and gently squared

Sea salt and freshly ground black pepper

¼ cup grapeseed oil

2 tablespoons diced shallot

2 heirloom apples, such as Cox's Orange Pippin, Newtown Pippin, Roxbury Russet, or real Granny Smiths, peeled, cored, and sliced

1 tablespoon Riesling vinegar or other good-quality white wine vinegar

2 tablespoons chopped fresh chervil

2 tablespoons chopped flat-leaf parsley

To make the puree: Bring the apples, water, apple juice, cream, and rosemary to a very slow simmer in a saucepan over medium-low heat. Cook for 5 to 7 minutes, or until the apples soften but are not mushy.

Drain the apples through a colander. Set aside for at least 10 minutes to ensure the apples drain completely. Reserve the drained liquid.

Discard the rosemary stem, but don't worry if a few small leaves or needles remain. Transfer the apples with the butter to a blender or the bowl of a food processor fitted with the metal blade and puree until smooth. Add some of the reserved cooking liquid to thin out the puree, if necessary. Season the puree with salt and pepper. Set aside, covered, to keep warm.

To cook the trout: Season the trout with salt and pepper.

Heat 2 tablespoons of the oil in a heavy-bottomed skillet, large enough to hold half of the fillets, over medium-high heat. Sear the fillets, skin side down, for about 5 minutes, or until cooked through. Transfer to a warm platter. Repeat with the remaining fillets, adding more oil as needed.

Lightly blot most of the excess oil from the pan. Reduce the heat to medium-low. Add the shallot. Cook for 1 to 2 minutes, or until it begins to soften. Add the apple slices. Cook for 2 to 3 minutes, or until warmed through. Add the vinegar. Remove the skillet from the heat. Stir in the chervil and parsley. Season lightly with salt and pepper.

To serve, divide the puree among 4 warmed plates. Put a fillet, skin side up, on top of the puree. Top each fillet with the apples. Top each with a second fillet and serve.

LINE-CAUGHT CHATHAM COD CAKES

In the early days of cod fishing, the Atlantic waters off New England were so populated with codfish that sailors and fishermen could never have imagined they would one day face extinction. Fishermen spent months at sea, bringing home huge amounts of cod. Because their ships had no refrigeration, they salted and dried the fish as soon as it was caught. This meant creative cooks from Maine down the coast had to devise ways to prepare the valuable catch, and cod cakes were a favorite.

Today, factory trawlers wreak environmental havoc on the remaining cod supply. Their methods pick up so much bycatch that a lot more than just cod die. Hook-and-line-caught cod, on the other hand, is sustainable. It's a challenge to find line-caught fish, but it's worth the trouble. Look for it in fish markets that sell wild-caught salmon and sustainably farmed shrimp. Not only will you put a good piece of cod on the family table, you will also support an artisan fishing culture that once guaranteed the survival of numerous New England communities and could one day do so again. Cod cakes with fresh cod are easier to make than salt cod cakes, as the fresh fish is easier to handle—and you will be keeping a lid on your sodium intake.

Makes 8 cod cakes; serves 4

2 TABLESPOONS COARSE SEA SALT

1½ POUNDS YUKON GOLD OR COROLLA POTATOES, PEELED AND CUT INTO 2" CHUNKS

1½ POUNDS BONELESS, SKINLESS COD FILLETS, CUT INTO 1½" CUBES

2 TABLESPOONS GRATED ONION

2 TABLESPOONS UNSALTED BUTTER, AT ROOM TEMPERATURE

1 TABLESPOON FINELY CHOPPED FLAT-LEAF PARSLEY

1 TABLESPOON FINELY CHOPPED FRESH CHERVIL, DILL, OR ADDITIONAL FLAT-LEAF PARSLEY (IF YOU CANNOT FIND CHERVIL OR DILL)

1 TABLESPOON FINELY CHOPPED FRESH CHIVES

1 LARGE ORGANIC EGG + 1 LARGE ORGANIC EGG YOLK

1–2 CUPS COARSE FRESH BREAD CRUMBS (SEE NOTE)

¼ CUP GRAPESEED OIL

Fill a large pot about halfway with water and add the salt. Add the potatoes and bring to a boil. Reduce the heat and simmer briskly for 25 to 35 minutes, or until the potatoes are nearly tender. Add the cod. Return to a simmer and cook, partially covered, for about 6 minutes longer, or until the fish is soft. Drain well. Transfer both the fish and potatoes to a colander to cool for 8 to 10 minutes.

When cool, transfer to a large mixing bowl. Add the onion, butter, herbs, egg, and egg yolk. With your hands or a potato masher, mash the mixture until thoroughly mixed. You will have about 6 cups. Form the mixture into 8 patties about 4" across.

Spread the bread crumbs in a shallow dish. Dip the patties in the crumbs to coat both sides. Use care, as the patties will be delicate.

Heat 2 tablespoons of the oil until hot in a large skillet over medium-high heat. Fry the patties for 4 to 5 minutes on each side, or until golden brown and heated all the way through. You will have to do this in batches. Wipe the crumbs from the pan between batches, and add more oil as needed. Drain on paper towels before serving.

Note : TO MAKE THE BREAD CRUMBS, WHIZ 4 SLICES OF COUNTRY-STYLE OR ARTISAN BREAD IN A FOOD PROCESSOR OR BLENDER.

SOFT-SHELL CRAB SANDWICH

I would like to find whoever "invented" the soft-shell crab sandwich and give that person a massive hug. This is one tasty sandwich! Soft-shell crabs are meant to be eaten whole, shells and all. I find there is something about putting them between two slices of home-baked bread and adding some greens and dressing that takes them to a whole nother place. Make each sandwich with one or two crabs (depending on their size), flavor the bread with a little mustard and mayonnaise, and top it with the Apple Slaw on page 226 and a few arugula leaves. What a delicious contrast between succulent, crispy crab, the sweetish slaw, and the beautifully sharp pepperiness of arugula.

Serves 6

12 live Maryland soft-shell crabs

2 cups unbleached all-purpose flour

¼ cup minced fresh thyme

Sea salt and freshly ground black pepper

¼ cup unsalted butter

12 slices Old-Fashioned Honey Wheat Bread (page 12) or your favorite whole wheat bread

3 tablespoons mayonnaise

2 tablespoons grainy mustard

1 cup arugula

1½ cups Apple Slaw (page 226)

Remove the crabs' soft, featherlike gills by lifting each side of the shell and pulling it off with your fingers or snipping with kitchen shears. Use kitchen shears to remove the eyes and mouth of each crab. Dry the crabs well with a clean kitchen towel.

Mix together the flour and thyme in a clean paper bag. Add salt and pepper to taste. One at a time, put the crabs in the bag with the seasoned flour. Shake until well coated.

Heat a large skillet over medium-high heat. When hot, add the butter. As soon as the butter melts, add the crabs. Cook for about 4 minutes on each side, or until nicely browned. Transfer to a warm platter lined with a clean kitchen towel.

Toast the bread slices under a hot broiler or in a toaster oven.

Stir together the mayonnaise and mustard in a small bowl. Spread the mayonnaise on each slice of toast. Divide the arugula and layer it over 6 slices of toast. Top the arugula with the slaw, followed by 2 crabs per sandwich. Top with the remaining slices of toast and serve.

LINE-CAUGHT CHATHAM COD CAKE SANDWICH

You know how remarkable a good fish sandwich can be, and a cod cake sandwich is about as good as it gets—it vies with the Soft-Shell Crab Sandwich (page 140) as my favorite! Cod cakes themselves are so rewarding and delicious, you will make them for dinner or even for hors d'oeuvres.

Makes 4 sandwiches

1 TABLESPOON FINELY SLICED FRESH CHIVES

¼ CUP MAYONNAISE

1 CUP TORN DANDELION GREENS

1 CUP TORN ARUGULA

¼ CUP TORN FRISÉE

¼ CUP SHAVED RED ONION

¼ CUP GRATED SWEET CARROTS

1 TABLESPOON FRESHLY GRATED ORANGE ZEST

2 TABLESPOONS EXTRA-VIRGIN OLIVE OIL

2 TABLESPOONS WHITE BALSAMIC VINEGAR

SEA SALT AND FRESHLY GROUND BLACK PEPPER

8 SLICES OLD-FASHIONED HONEY-WHEAT BREAD (PAGE 12)
   OR GOOD-QUALITY POTATO ROLLS, SPLIT

1–2 TABLESPOONS GRAPESEED OIL

4 LINE-CAUGHT CHATHAM COD CAKES (PAGE 136)

Stir the chives into the mayonnaise in a small bowl.

Toss the dandelion greens, arugula, frisée, onion, carrots, and orange zest in a mixing bowl. Add the oil and vinegar and toss well. Season to taste with salt and pepper.

Toast the bread or rolls under a preheated broiler or in a toaster oven. Spread 4 slices of bread or the bottom half of each roll with the chive mayonnaise.

Heat 1 tablespoon of the oil in a skillet over medium-high heat. Reheat the cod cakes in the hot skillet, pressing on them with the back of a large spoon or a spatula to flatten them a little. Turn once or twice to ensure the cod cakes are heated through. Add more oil if needed.

Put a cod cake on 1 of the prepared slices of bread or roll halves. Top each cod cake with some of the salad mix and then with the remaining bread or top roll. Serve any extra salad on the side.

CORNMEAL CATFISH

In the spring, my family used to go to my uncle's place on the Mississippi River to help during flood season. When the water rose high enough, we could fish for catfish in the backyard. Uncle Marvin fired up a drum grill, and he and my mom cooked the fish in big cast-iron skillets. We ate them with tartar sauce, skillet-cooked fried mashed potatoes, and raw veggies sitting in ice water.

This recipe is a regional southern dish, in which the flavor of the toasted corn in the cornmeal is remarkable with the catfish: oily, earthy, and toasty. Catfish are an important part of a healthy ecosystem, as they are prolific and thrive in just about any body of fresh water. And, like trout, catfish can be sustainably farmed successfully. Eating catfish is almost like Old Man River is feeding you; you can taste the spirit of the river in the fish. Some folks think they taste a little fishy, but I say rather than trying to find fish that doesn't "taste like fish," which can lead to overfishing of varieties like cod and halibut, learn to appreciate fish that taste like fish! Just make sure it's really, really fresh.

Serves 6

2 TABLESPOONS RAW SUGAR

1 TABLESPOON SEA SALT

1 TABLESPOON FINELY CHOPPED FRESH THYME

1 TABLESPOON FINELY CHOPPED FRESH SAGE

1 TABLESPOON FINELY GRATED LEMON ZEST

6 BONELESS, SKINLESS CATFISH FILLETS (ABOUT 2 POUNDS)

1 CUP SPELT OR UNBLEACHED OR ALL-PURPOSE FLOUR

1 CUP WHOLE MILK

2 CUPS FINE STONEGROUND CORNMEAL

2 CUPS GRAPESEED OIL

Mix together the sugar, salt, thyme, sage, and lemon zest in a small bowl. Coat the catfish fillets with the mixture. Transfer to a glass or sturdy plastic dish, cover, and refrigerate for 2 hours.

Lightly rinse the fillets to remove most of the herb mixture. Blot dry with a clean kitchen towel.

Spread the flour in a shallow dish, pour the milk in another, and spread the cornmeal in a third. Dip the fillets in the flour. Pat off the excess, then dip the fillets in the milk. Finally, dip the fillets in the cornmeal to coat both sides.

Heat the grapeseed oil in a deep, heavy-bottomed skillet over medium heat. When the oil is hot and shimmering, cook the fillets for 3 minutes on 1 side. Turn and cook for 3 to 4 minutes longer, or until lightly browned. You may want to do this in batches. Transfer the fillets to a clean kitchen towel to drain. Serve immediately.

ALBACORE TUNA MELT

Everyone has had a tuna melt at a diner or coffee shop; my version, made with albacore tuna, is better than anything you have had before yet still evokes the beloved original.

Albacore is considered a sustainable tuna, partly because it does not get as large as other tuna and therefore does not have time to gather as much mercury. Albacore is not quite as flavorful or bright red, nor does it have as thick a layer of belly fat as its relatives the big-eye, yellowfin or bluefin tuna. For those reasons, it is less prized by Asian fish-eating cultures, which also helps to keep the fish sustainable. It's a wonderful fish that does well with strong flavors. I finish it off with an easy-to-make sage mayo, although you could use a different herb to change the character of the recipe a little.

Serves 4

1 TABLESPOON GRAPESEED OIL

¼ CUP DICED BACON (ABOUT 1 OUNCE)

2 TABLESPOONS DICED FRESH SHALLOT OR ONION

1 POUND FRESH ALBACORE TUNA, CUT INTO ½" DICE
(ABOUT 2 CUPS)

KOSHER SALT AND FRESHLY GROUND BLACK PEPPER

¾ CUPS SAGE MAYONNAISE (OPPOSITE PAGE)

½ CUP FINELY DICED CELERY

1–2 TABLESPOONS FRESH LEMON JUICE

4 SLICES SOURDOUGH BREAD, ½"–¾" THICK, TOASTED

4 SLICES MILD COW'S MILK OR SHEEP'S MILK CHEESE

Heat the oil in a medium skillet over medium heat. Add the bacon and shallot. Cook for 3 to 4 minutes, or until nicely browned.

Drain some of the fat from the pan. Add the diced tuna and season lightly with salt and pepper. Cook for 3 to 4 minutes, or until well seared but not fully cooked. Remove the pan from the heat and set aside to cool slightly.

Mix together the mayonnaise, celery, and lemon juice in a medium mixing bowl. Add the tuna, onion, and bacon. Mix well. Season to taste with salt and pepper. Divide the tuna salad among the toast slices.

Top the tuna with the cheese. Broil until the cheese is melted and lightly browned. Serve immediately.

SAGE MAYONNAISE

Makes about 1⅔ cups

3 LARGE EGG YOLKS

1 LARGE EGG

3 TABLESPOONS SLICED FRESH SAGE (OR YOUR FAVORITE HERB)

2 TABLESPOONS WHITE VINEGAR

2 TABLESPOONS GRAINY MUSTARD

1–2 TEASPOONS LOCAL HONEY

¾ CUP EXTRA-VIRGIN OLIVE OIL

1–2 TABLESPOONS FRESH LEMON JUICE

KOSHER SALT AND FRESHLY GROUND BLACK PEPPER

Combine the egg yolks, egg, sage, vinegar, mustard, and 1 teaspoon of the honey in a mixing bowl. Whisk vigorously until well mixed.

While whisking briskly, slowly add the oil, a few drips at a time. When about half of the oil has been absorbed, add the rest in a steady stream, whisking constantly. Alternatively, make the mayonnaise in the bowl of a food processor fitted with the metal blade. With the motor running, add the oil through the tube until emulsified. If you make the mayonnaise in the food processor, you might choose to stir in the herbs after the mayonnaise is made.

Thin the mayonnaise with lemon juice, if necessary. Season with salt and pepper. Sweeten with more honey, if needed.

SEARED WILD STRIPED BASS
with TOMATO SAGE "FONDUE"

Wild striped bass is one of the more recent success stories from the sustainable seafood move-ment. Once prolific along the eastern seaboard of the United States, striped bass were at a time so depleted that even sport fishermen had trouble finding and catching a single fish. The alarm was sounded and moratoriums were imposed. While many, including chefs, objected at first, the bass stock has since replenished itself. Now there are solid fishery-management practices in place that are monitored and enforced with happy results.

The recipe below is a testament to why we should be forever vigilant in making sure the striped bass population is never again diminished. Like many fish dishes, it's very simple to prepare and yet incredibly tasty. I take full advantage of the fact that striped bass season overlaps with the tomato season here in Connecticut: a culinary match made in heaven!

Serves 6

2 TABLESPOONS ROASTED GARLIC CLOVES (4–5 CLOVES)

2 TABLESPOONS SLICED FRESH SAGE

SEA SALT

6 SKIN-ON STRIPED BASS FILLETS (EACH ABOUT 6 OUNCES)

2 TABLESPOONS GRAPESEED OIL

2 TABLESPOONS DICED SHALLOT

2 TABLESPOONS UNSALTED BUTTER, SOFTENED

4 HEIRLOOM TOMATOES, PREFERABLY 2 OR 3 VARIETIES
   (ABOUT 2 POUNDS), CORED AND SLICED ¼" THICK

2 TABLESPOONS COLD UNSALTED BUTTER, CUT INTO ½" CUBES

2 TEASPOONS EXTRA-VIRGIN OLIVE OIL

¼ CUP FRESH HERB LEAVES, SUCH AS CHERVIL, PARSLEY,
   OR YOUNG CARROT TOPS

Smash the garlic, sage, and ½ teaspoon of salt together using a mortar and pestle or the broad side of a knife on a cutting board until combined and fragrant.

Season the fillets with sea salt and then heat a large skillet over medium-high heat. When hot, add the grapeseed oil and immediately add the fillets, skin side down. Lightly press each fillet to ensure that the skin makes contact with the hot pan. Cook for 3 to 5 minutes, or until the flesh nearest the bottom of the pan turns white and the skin browns.

Use a thin spatula to turn the fillets over. Add the shallot and softened butter to one side of the pan while tilting the pan toward you slightly. The butter will immediately melt and bubble and collect with the shallot in the nook of the pan closest to you. Use a large spoon to baste the fillets with the butter and shallot. Continue basting for about 2 minutes, lifting the fillets gently so that the butter seeps under them. Transfer the fillets to a warm, ovenproof platter. Check the doneness of the fillets. If they need a little more cooking, put the platter in a 250°F oven for 2 to 3 minutes. The bass should be cooked through but not overcooked.

Reduce the heat to medium-low. Add the tomato slices, cold butter, and garlic-sage paste. Cook at a simmer for 4 to 5 minutes, gently moving the ingredients around the pan with a wooden spoon to distribute the butter and garlic paste evenly, until the sauce comes together as a thickened mixture.

To serve, spoon the fondue on a warm serving platter and set the fillets on top of the fondue. Drizzle with olive oil for serving. Garnish with the herbs.

Chapter 5

MAIN COURSE AMERICA

When it comes to the main course, people like to strut their stuff. This is the part of the meal where we usually spend the most time and energy, and, over time, main courses may become "signature dishes." While fish often is the main course, we Americans usually think meat or poultry when we plan a meal. Consider family parties or neighborhood potlucks where you know you will be treated to Uncle Roy's smothered pork chops, Sally's lasagna, or Grandma's pot roast. How they cook their favorites becomes part of these people's identities, as is reflected in cook-offs at county and state fairs across the country. In my family when I was growing up, we looked forward to my mom's fried chicken.

Balance is important when it comes to the main event. There should always be more vegetables than protein or starch on the plate, but all three elements are crucial to a good meal. I have attempted to provide really good choices for accompaniments to the main courses in Chapter 6, Side Dishes. Also, a number of the dishes in this chapter are self-contained, such as Lamb and Whole Grain Stew (page 183) and Braised Short Ribs with Creamy Cheese Grits (page 173). To be honest, this makes life easier. My hope is that in this collection of main courses you will find one or two that you can "own" and which you will start making as part of your own family celebrations. This is how heirloom recipes get started.

HOMEGROWN FRIED CHICKEN

CHICKEN POT PIE

CHICKEN OR TURKEY À LA KING

SMOTHERED PORK CHOPS

PORK LOIN ROAST WITH DRIED FRUITS AND APPLE CIDER

SCOTT COUNTY, MISSOURI–STYLE DRY RIBS

(continued)

Meat Loaf

Beef Short-Rib Pot Roast

Braised Short Ribs with Creamy Cheese Grits

Shredded Beef Chili

Leg of Pasture-Raised Lamb
Stuffed with Chestnuts
and Dried Cranberries

Lamb and Whole Grain Stew

Sweet Pea and Lemon-Ricotta Ravioli

Macaroni and Cheese

HOMEGROWN FRIED CHICKEN

Like most fried foods, when done correctly, fried chicken is not bad for you. It should be enjoyed in moderation, but when you feel the urge to fry up some chicken, do it right. You won't be sorry: It's sublime! I learned to fry chicken from my mother, who learned from her mother-in-law. It's a cooking technique that requires some trial and error; you will probably have a few failures before success, but when you do, you will know why American fried chicken is famous around the world. People used to cook more by feel and aroma than specific recipes, and fried chicken fits into this matrix. There are a few things to keep in mind: The hot fat (and yes, I use lard) should come about halfway up the chicken, and while you can turn the chicken any number of times for even cooking, keep the lid on it between turnings. This keeps the chicken in contact with the bottom of the pan, which is important. The milk brine provides a little tang and also helps the flour stay on the chicken.

Serves 4

MILK BRINE

2 quarts whole milk

1 onion, chopped

3–4 garlic heads, hit once with a hammer or the side of a heavy knife

3 tablespoons fresh thyme

Kosher salt and freshly ground black pepper

1 (2–3-pound) chicken, cut into 8 pieces

FLOUR MIX

2 cups all-purpose flour

1 tablespoon onion powder

1 tablespoon garlic powder

1 tablespoon fresh thyme

1 teaspoon toasted, ground yellow mustard seeds

Kosher salt and freshly ground black pepper

FRYING

½ cup lard

½ cup (1 stick) butter

(continued)

To make the brine: Bring 1 quart of milk to a simmer in a saucepan over medium-high heat. Remove the pan from the heat. Add the onion, garlic, and thyme. Set aside to come to room temperature. Season to taste with salt and pepper, using enough salt so that the milk tastes a little like seawater.

When the milk is nearly cool, stir in the remaining 1 quart cold milk. Transfer the milk brine to a dish large enough to hold the chicken pieces. Add the chicken, cover, and refrigerate for at least 2 hours and up to 4 hours. Drain the chicken, discard the brine, and pat the chicken dry.

To make the flour mix: Mix together the flour, onion powder, garlic powder, thyme, and mustard seeds in a shallow dish. Season with salt and pepper.

Put the chicken pieces in the flour. Turn to coat. Let the coated chicken pieces sit for 10 to 15 minutes.

To fry the chicken: Heat a large, heavy skillet over medium-high heat. When hot, heat the lard until liquid and so hot it is nearly smoking. Add the butter to the skillet. Using tongs, lay the chicken pieces in the hot fat, which should come about halfway up the sides of the chicken.

Cover the skillet. Let the chicken fry for 3 to 4 minutes, then turn the chicken pieces. Watch the chicken carefully, turning as needed to brown evenly on both sides and cook through, about 25 to 30 minutes total. (The smaller pieces might be cooked through in 20 minutes.) Adjust the heat if necessary to prevent scorching, but try to keep it as high as you can.

Lift the chicken pieces from the hot fat as they are cooked. Drain on clean kitchen towels or paper towels. Serve hot.

CHICKEN POT PIE

You may be surprised to learn that chicken used to be relatively expensive, and fried chicken and other chicken dishes were served with plenty of vegetables to stretch out the meal. These days, chicken is inexpensive, and we tend to load our plates with meat rather than vegetables. Try going back to the old ways. It's better for you.

My mom used to haggle with the butcher and buy 5 or 6 chickens at once. She would come home and put the chickens in a big pot to make broth. We ate chicken all week: chicken pot pie, chicken à la king, and chicken soup. This is best when made in the morning and allowed to sit and thicken for a few hours before being reheated and served.

Serves 4

CHICKEN

1 (3–3½-POUND) CHICKEN

1 BAY LEAF

⅔ CUP PEELED, DICED CARROTS (2 CARROTS)

⅔ CUP DICED CELERY (2 RIBS)

⅔ CUP PEELED, DICED CELERY ROOT (ABOUT ⅓ OF A BULB)

⅔ CUP DICED ONION (1 SMALL ONION)

2 TABLESPOONS CHOPPED FRESH THYME

1 TABLESPOON CHOPPED FRESH ROSEMARY

SAUCE

½ CUP PEELED, DICED CELERY ROOT (ABOUT ¼ OF A BULB)

½ CUP PEELED, DICED PARSNIP (1 PARSNIP)

½ CUP PEELED, DICED POTATO (1 SMALL POTATO)

½ CUP HEAVY CREAM

SEA SALT AND FRESHLY GROUND BLACK PEPPER

PASTRY

2 CUPS UNBLEACHED ALL-PURPOSE FLOUR

2 TEASPOONS KOSHER SALT

2 TABLESPOONS CHOPPED FRESH THYME

½ CUP COLD UNSALTED BUTTER, CUT INTO PIECES

½ CUP (¼ POUND) COLD LARD, CUT INTO PIECES

5–6 TABLESPOONS ICE WATER

To cook the chicken: Put the whole chicken in a large stockpot and cover with water. Add the bay leaf and bring the water to a low simmer over medium-low heat. Do not let the water boil. Adjust the heat lower to maintain a gentle simmer. Skim any foam that rises to the surface. Poach the chicken, partially covered, for about 1 hour, or until it is cooked through and begins to pull away from the bones.

After the chicken has been poaching for about 30 minutes, add the carrots, celery, celery root, onion, thyme, and rosemary.

When the chicken is cooked, lift the chicken from the water and set aside to cool. Using a slotted spoon, remove the vegetables from the stock and set aside to use later. Skim any fat from the surface of the stock with a metal spoon.

To make the sauce: Bring the stock to a rapid simmer over medium-high heat. Add the celery root, parsnip, and potato. Cook for about 1 hour, or until the stock reduces to about $1\frac{1}{2}$ quarts (6 cups) and the vegetables soften. Discard the bay leaf. Transfer the stock and vegetables to a blender and puree until smooth. You may have to do this in batches. Alternatively, puree the sauce with an immersion blender directly in the pot.

As the stock is pureed, pour it into a bowl. When all is in the bowl, stir in the cream. Season to taste with salt and pepper.

Meanwhile, remove and discard the skin from the chicken and pull the meat from the bones. Cut or tear the meat into bite-size pieces and add to the gravy. You will have about 4 cups of pulled chicken. Stir in the reserved vegetables.

To make the pastry: Mix together the flour, salt, and thyme in a large bowl. Add the pieces of butter and lard. Working with your fingers, 2 forks, or 2 knives, blend the fat into the flour until the mixture resembles coarse crumbs. Sprinkle with 4 to 5 tablespoons of ice water. Mix just until the pastry comes together. Add a touch more water, if necessary.

Turn out the dough onto a lightly floured surface and pat into a disc. Wrap the dough in plastic and refrigerate for about 1 hour and up to 6 hours, or until thoroughly chilled.

Preheat the oven to 375°F.

On a lightly floured surface, roll the dough into a circle or square about 1" larger than the diameter of the baking dish you are using.

Spoon the chicken and gravy into a 2- to $2\frac{1}{2}$-quart baking dish. Lay the dough over the top of the chicken filling and crimp the edges of the dough around the rim of the casserole. Cut a small steam vent in the crust. Bake for about 1 hour, or until heated through and the crust is golden brown. Serve hot.

CHICKEN *or* TURKEY À LA KING

I think of this old-fashioned-sounding dish as a deconstructed pot pie. It has the same elements without the pastry, although the toast it's spooned over accomplishes much the same thing: It absorbs a lot of the gravy and gives the dish some crunch. Be sure to toast the bread all the way through, as you don't want it soft and bready in the center. In a pop-up toaster, this might require 2 toasting cycles. If you pan-toast the bread, let it get nice and crispy on both sides. Spread the hot toast with a little butter.

Chicken à la king is one of those old-time recipes that should be embraced again. It's that good! My mom used to make it with peas from the garden, either fresh off the vine or that she had frozen earlier in the year. She cut the other vegetables so that they were approximately the same size as the peas, and the effect was confetti on the plate. This is also a terrific way to use leftover roasted vegetables.

Serves 2 to 4

½ CUP CUBED POTATOES

2 TEASPOONS OLIVE OIL

⅓ CUP SLICED WILTED GREENS, SUCH AS SPINACH, OR BLANCHED AND SHOCKED BROCCOLI FLORETS (ABOUT 2 OUNCES)

2 CUPS CHICKEN STOCK, PREFERABLY HOMEMADE

2 CUPS CHOPPED OR SHREDDED LEFTOVER CHICKEN OR TURKEY MEAT

½ CUP ROASTED CARROTS (PAGE 4), CUT INTO ¼" CUBES

½ CUP PEAS, FRESH OR FROZEN

½ CUP CUBED ROASTED PARSNIPS (PAGE 4), CUT INTO ¼" CUBES

½ CUP HEAVY CREAM

1 TABLESPOON FRESH THYME

KOSHER SALT AND FRESHLY GROUND BLACK PEPPER

2–4 SLICES TOASTED BREAD, ¾" THICK, BUTTERED

Cover the potatoes with lightly salted water in a small saucepan. Bring to a boil over medium-high heat. Reduce the heat. Simmer for about 15 minutes, or until tender when pierced with a fork. Alternatively, you can use leftover roasted potatoes for this recipe.

Heat the oil in a large skillet over medium-high heat. When hot, add the greens and cook, stirring, for 1 to 2 minutes, or until the greens wilt. Transfer to a cutting board and cut into bite-size pieces. You should have ⅓ cup of greens.

Heat the stock to a simmer in a large saucepan over medium heat. Transfer to a blender or the bowl of a food processor fitted with the metal blade. Add the potatoes and process for 30 to 60 seconds, or until smooth. Return to the saucepan and bring back to a simmer. Cook for 3 to 5 minutes, or until the stock resembles light gravy.

Add the meat, carrots, peas, parsnips, and greens. Bring to a simmer and cook for about 5 minutes. Stir in the cream and thyme until well combined. Season to taste with salt and pepper.

To serve, put a warm slice of buttered toast in the center of each of 2 to 4 warm plates. Spoon the chicken à la king over the toast.

HERITAGE TURKEY

AMERICA'S MISGUIDED CRAVING FOR MORE AND MORE WHITE TURKEY MEAT NEARLY DID IN THE OLD-FASHIONED THANKSGIVING TURKEY. TO MEET DEMAND, MASS-MARKET TURKEY FARMERS GENETICALLY MODIFIED THE BIRDS SO THAT THEIR BREASTS BECAME SO LARGE THAT THEY COULD BARELY STAND, MUCH LESS FLY OR BREED NATURALLY. THANKS TO THE DEDICATION OF CONCERNED FARMERS AND SHOW-BIRD BREEDERS, HERITAGE TURKEYS ARE ONCE AGAIN AVAILABLE TO THOSE WHO SEEK THEM OUT. THE NEXT TIME YOU BUY A TURKEY, ASK THE BUTCHER WHERE AND HOW IT WAS RAISED, AND TRY TO BUY A HERITAGE BREED, SUCH AS A STANDARD BRONZE, NARRAGANSETT, JERSEY BUFF, OR BOURBON RED. NOT ONLY WILL YOU BE COOKING A RESPONSIBLY RAISED BIRD, IT WILL TASTE BETTER TOO.

SMOTHERED PORK CHOPS

My family always made use of the local meat locker, a place where you could store large cuts of meat and have the on-site butchers cut the meat. I remember being surprised when my mom asked the butcher to cut her some 1"-thick pork chops "from the butt." Mom had been teaching me how to cook since I was very young, so I was pretty sure I knew where chops came from, and it wasn't the butt. She told me that for some reason she "couldn't explain," the shoulder was called the butt.

When you look at a shoulder chop with its crisscrossed bones, you might wonder how you'll ever eat it. But follow this recipe: The results are amazing, as rich and deeply comforting a braised dish as you might hope to eat, meat literally smothered with gravy and onions. Onions are key, and while some recipes for smothered pork chops and chicken include bell peppers, mushrooms, and perhaps some other ingredients, there are always onions. If I were a pork chop and had to choose a way to go, I would choose smothering! Serve with Collard Greens (page 214).

Serves 4

- 4 shoulder pork chops, each about 1" thick, trimmed (about 1 pound)
- ¼ teaspoon salt (optional)
- ⅛ teaspoon freshly ground black pepper
- 2 tablespoons all-purpose flour
- 2 tablespoons grapeseed or canola oil
- 2 yellow onions, cut into ¼" slices
- 3 green bell peppers, seeded and cut into ¼" slices
- 3 cups low-sodium chicken broth
- Slivered parsley leaves for garnish

Preheat the oven to 300°F. Season each chop with the salt, if using, and black pepper. Pour 1 tablespoon of the flour onto a plate. Dip each chop into the flour and shake off the excess.

Heat the oil in a heavy, ovenproof skillet over medium heat. Put the pork chops in the skillet. Cook until they are well browned, about 4 minutes per side. Remove the chops from the skillet and set aside.

Add the onions and bell peppers to the skillet. Increase the heat to medium-high. Sprinkle the remaining 1 tablespoon of flour over the vegetables and cook, stirring constantly for 5 minutes, or until the vegetables are brown.

Remove the skillet from the heat. Gradually stir in the broth. Cook and stir until the sauce is slightly thickened and smooth. Bury the chops in the gravy. Cover the skillet and transfer to the oven. Cook for 2 hours, or until the pork is tender. To serve, divide the pork chops among 4 plates and spoon gravy over each serving. Garnish with the herbs.

PORK LOIN ROAST *with* DRIED FRUITS *and* APPLE CIDER

Good, well-raised pork is one of the best meats you can eat, both in terms of taste and healthful-ness, and it's decidedly no longer necessary to cook pork until it's dry and gray. To the contrary, it's preferable for the meat to be just a little pink and moist in the center. The sauce for this pork is filled with plump dried fruit, which marries well with the sweet meat, and it's also great spooned over Heirloom Mashed Potatoes on page 211.

Serves 4

MARINADE

¼ CUP OLIVE OIL

2 TABLESPOONS ORGANIC APPLE CIDER

6 GARLIC CLOVES, MINCED

2 TABLESPOONS COARSELY CHOPPED FRESH THYME

2 TABLESPOONS COARSELY CHOPPED FRESH ROSEMARY

2 TABLESPOONS COARSELY CHOPPED FRESH SAGE

2 TABLESPOONS COARSELY CHOPPED FLAT-LEAF PARSLEY

SEA SALT AND FRESHLY GROUND BLACK PEPPER

ROAST

1 (2½–3-POUND) PORK LOIN, PREFERABLY HEIRLOOM PORK,
   TRIMMED OF ANY FAT OR SILVER SKIN

SEA SALT AND FRESHLY GROUND BLACK PEPPER

¼ CUP GRAPESEED OIL

2 TABLESPOONS UNSALTED BUTTER

¼–⅓ CUP DIJON MUSTARD

SAUCE

3 CUPS CHICKEN STOCK, PREFERABLY HOMEMADE

2 CUPS ORGANIC APPLE CIDER

SEA SALT AND FRESHLY GROUND BLACK PEPPER

5–6 TABLESPOONS UNSALTED BUTTER

1 ONION, COARSELY CHOPPED

1 CUP DRIED SOUR CHERRIES

1 CUP DRIED APPLES, EACH SLICED LENGTHWISE INTO 4–5 PIECES

1 CUP DRIED APRICOTS, EACH SLICED LENGTHWISE INTO 4–5 PIECES

To make the marinade: Stir together the olive oil, cider, garlic, thyme, rosemary, sage, and parsley in a shallow glass, ceramic, or other nonreactive dish. Season to taste with salt and pepper.

Lay the trimmed pork in the marinade and turn the meat so it is coated on all sides with the marinade. Cover and refrigerate for at least 2 hours and up to 12 hours.

To cook the roast: Preheat the oven to 350°F.

Remove the meat from the refrigerator. Leave on the countertop for about 30 minutes to reach room temperature. With a spoon, scrape the marinade from the roast and transfer to a small bowl. With a clean kitchen towel, wipe any residual marinade from the meat so that it is as dry as possible. Sprinkle the meat on all sides with salt and pepper.

Heat the grapeseed oil and butter in a roasting pan or large skillet over medium-high heat until the butter melts. Sear the roast on all sides for 2 to 3 minutes per side, using tongs to turn the meat.

Add the mustard to the bowl with the marinade. Use a brush to rub the roast with the marinade (the roast will be hot), covering as much of the meat as possible.

Set the roast on a rack in a roasting pan. Roast for about 1 hour, or until an instant-read thermometer registers 150°F to 155°F. Remove the roast from the oven, tent with foil, and let it rest for 20 minutes.

Meanwhile, make the sauce: Bring the stock to a boil in a saucepan over high heat. Reduce the heat to medium-high. Simmer briskly for 25 to 30 minutes, or until reduced to about 2 cups.

Bring the cider to a boil in another saucepan over high heat. Reduce the heat to medium-high. Simmer briskly for 20 to 25 minutes, or until reduced to about 1 cup. Add the cider to the stock. Season to taste with salt and pepper. Cover to keep warm and set aside.

Melt 2 tablespoons of the butter in a skillet over medium-high heat. Cook the onion for 5 to 8 minutes, or until softened. Pour the stock and cider into the skillet, scraping the bottom of the pan with a wooden spoon to deglaze. Add the cherries, apples, and apricots. Simmer for 5 to 10 minutes, or until the fruit plumps up and softens.

Add 3 tablespoons of the butter. Lower the heat to medium-low and stir until the butter is incorporated. Add the remaining 1 tablespoon of butter, if necessary, to thicken the sauce a little. Adjust the seasoning with salt and pepper.

To serve, slice the pork into $\frac{1}{4}$"-thick slices. Spoon the sauce over the pork, or pass it at the table.

SCOTT COUNTY, MISSOURI-STYLE DRY RIBS

"Ribs, salt, pepper, and broth." That's what my mom told anyone who asked her how she cooked ribs. She was from the Bootheel of Missouri, the southeastern end known more for baking, roasting, smothering, and frying than for smoking, rubbing, and saucing, but that didn't stop her from turning out the best ribs I have ever had.

She prepared them very simply. Instead of precooking the ribs, she simply seasoned them with salt and pepper and laid them straight on a grill over slow-burning coals. As the ribs cooked, she turned them periodically and basted them with ham-hock stock (Mom called it broth) and occasionally resalted them. After 45 minutes to an hour, they were tender and ready to eat. When you don't steam, poach, or smoke them, the flavor concentrates so that all you taste is pure pork.

Very rarely do I tweak my mom's recipes, but in this case I made an exception. A gentle, respectful application of finely grated lemon zest and sliced fresh chives at the end actually brings these ribs to a whole nother place. You will love them a whole lot.

Serves 2 or 3

1 FULL RACK BABY BACK RIBS, CUT INTO 4 PORTIONS

2 CUPS CHICKEN STOCK OR RICH HAM-HOCK STOCK, PREFERABLY HOMEMADE

KOSHER SALT AND FRESHLY GROUND BLACK PEPPER

3 TABLESPOONS FRESHLY GRATED LEMON ZEST

3 TABLESPOONS SLICED FRESH CHIVES

Prepare a gas or charcoal grill for indirect cooking. For a gas grill, this means turning one side of the burners on high and the other on medium. For a charcoal grill, mound all the hardwood charcoal on one side of the grill so that the ribs can be cooked over both hotter and cooler parts of the grill. Light the coals. Allow them to become white-hot.

Let the ribs sit on the counter until they reach room temperature. Baste them with the stock and put them on the hot side of the grill. Sear for 2 to 3 minutes on each side, or until they begin to turn brown.

Move the ribs to the cooler side of the grill. Cook for 3 to 4 minutes. Turn, baste with more stock, and sprinkle with salt and pepper. Repeat this turning, basting, and seasoning for about 1 hour to 1 hour 20 minutes, or until the meat begins to sag off of the ribs when you pick them up to turn. At this point you will have to treat them more carefully because of the softening meat. The goal is to glaze the ribs with the ham-hock stock while equalizing the smokiness from the coals with the saltiness of the ribs.

Garnish with the lemon zest and chives.

MEAT LOAF

Meat loaf, made well, is one of America's triumphs and demonstrates what resourceful home cooks can do. The glory of a good meat loaf is that it's as tasty cold as it is hot—as anyone who has ever tasted a meat loaf sandwich knows only too well—and when it's made with outstanding meat, nothing beats it. I make it with high-quality ground beef, such as the pasture-raised beef sold by Niman Ranch as well as from good butchers. A budget meal to be proud of.

Because meat loaf is seasonless, I serve it with a simple tomato and herb salad dressed with extra-virgin olive oil and sea salt in the summer. In cold weather, I often serve it with caramelized onion gravy.

Serves 6 to 8

2–3 TABLESPOONS OLIVE OIL

1 CUP PEELED, DICED PARSNIPS (2–4 PARSNIPS)

¾ CUP PEELED, DICED CARROTS (ABOUT 2 CARROTS)

½ CUP PEELED, DICED CELERY ROOT

⅓ CUP DICED ONION

KOSHER SALT AND FRESHLY GROUND BLACK PEPPER

2 CUPS SOFT, FRESH BREAD CRUMBS (FROM ABOUT 4 SLICES
    OF HIGH-QUALITY BREAD)

1 CUP WHOLE MILK

2 LARGE EGGS

⅓ CUP KETCHUP

1 TABLESPOON KOSHER SALT

¼ TEASPOON FRESHLY GROUND BLACK PEPPER

3 POUNDS HIGH-QUALITY GROUND BEEF, PREFERABLY
    PASTURE-RAISED (SEE "PASTURE-RAISED BEEF" ON PAGE 170)

Preheat the oven to 375°F.

Heat the oil in a large skillet over medium-high heat. When hot, add the parsnips, carrots, celery root, and onion with a pinch of salt and pepper. Cook for 6 to 8 minutes, or until softened. Set aside for 10 to 15 minutes to cool slightly.

Mix together the bread crumbs, milk, eggs, ketchup, salt, and pepper in a large mixing bowl. Add the meat and cooked vegetables. Use a wooden spoon or your hands to mix well.

(continued)

Transfer the meat to an 8" or 9" square or round baking dish. Spread it into a loaf form that is slightly mounded in the middle.

Bake for about 1½ hours, or until the meat loaf is cooked all the way through. An instant-read thermometer inserted in the center of the loaf should read 145°F.

Serve the meat loaf from the pan. Slice into serving pieces about 1" thick.

PASTURE-RAISED BEEF

GRASS-FED BEEF IS LEANER THAN GRAIN-FED, BUT IT'S JUST AS TASTY. WE LIKE IT BECAUSE THE ANIMALS SPEND THEIR TIME GRAZING IN PASTURES WHERE THEIR PRIMARY DIET CONSISTS OF THE GROWING VEGETATION. THE CATTLE ARE NOT SHIPPED TO FEEDLOTS FOR THE FINAL 5 OR 6 MONTHS OF THEIR LIVES TO BE FED GRAIN DIETS TO FATTEN THEM UP AND PROMOTE MARBLING. INSTEAD, THE CATTLE STAY WITH THEIR HERD IN THE OPEN AND DON'T CONSUME TREMENDOUS STORES OF GRAIN PRODUCED BY MEGA-AGRIBUSINESS. NOT ONLY IS PASTURE-RAISED BEEF FARMING BETTER FOR THE ANIMALS, IT'S BETTER FOR THE ENVIRONMENT TOO.

AFTER 2 YEARS OF CONCERTED EFFORTS TO FIND A LOCAL PRODUCER OF GRASS-FED, GRASS-FINISHED CATTLE, WE LOCATED DAVID HUSE OF STONEBROOK FARM IN WERNERVILLE, NEW YORK. DAVID HAS A LONG TRADITION OF RAISING ANIMALS ON WELL-MANAGED PASTURES AND HAS NOW REACHED A LEVEL OF PRODUCTION THAT AFFORDS US A YEAR-ROUND SUPPLY OF HIGH-QUALITY, DELICIOUS BEEF.

BEEF SHORT-RIB POT ROAST

A good pot roast is all about braising correctly and carefully. When you brown the meat well and then cook it slowly, it contracts. When it cools, it relaxes and absorbs the flavor of the broth and vegetables. And because the meat has already contracted once, it does not do so again, so the luscious flavors remain in the meat when it is reheated. This explains why stews and braises always taste better the next day. For just this reason, I recommend making this pot roast the day before you plan to serve it. You won't go wrong! If you feel ambitious, remove a few of the more overcooked carrots and potatoes, puree them, and return them to the pot to thicken the gravy.

You accomplish two things when you make a pot roast. First, the aroma and taste of the dish alone take you happily home, regardless of where you eat it. Second, you are cooking a secondary cut of meat, which is good for the planet.

Serves 6

2 BONELESS BEEF SHORT RIBS, ABOUT 1 POUND EACH (SEE NOTE)

KOSHER SALT AND FRESHLY GROUND BLACK PEPPER

2 TABLESPOONS GRAPESEED OIL

2 CUPS DICED CARROTS (3–4 CARROTS)

2 CUPS DICED CELERY (3–4 RIBS)

2 CUPS DICED YELLOW ONION (1 LARGE ONION)

2 CUPS DICED PARSNIPS (4 PARSNIPS)

2 QUARTS BEEF STOCK, PREFERABLY HOMEMADE

1 CUP DICED TOMATO, FRESH OR CANNED, DRAINED

Let the meat come to room temperature. Sprinkle on all sides with salt and pepper.

Preheat the oven to 300°F.

Heat the oil in a large flameproof baking pan or skillet over medium heat. When hot, sear the meat on one side for 2 to 3 minutes, or until nicely browned. Turn and sear all sides of the roast until nicely browned. Take your time when doing so. Remove the meat and set aside.

Add the carrots, celery, onion, and parsnips and cook, stirring, for 5 to 8 minutes, or until the vegetables are lightly browned. Transfer the cooked vegetables to a holding plate.

Note: YOU MAY HAVE TO SPECIAL ORDER BEEF SHORT RIBS, BUT YOUR BUTCHER SHOULD BE ABLE TO GET THEM QUITE EASILY. THEY ARE FLAT PIECES OF MEAT—LOOKING SOMETHING LIKE FLANK STEAKS—AND EACH WEIGHS ABOUT 1 POUND. YOU COULD SUBSTITUTE CHUCK ROAST OR EYE ROUND. MANY SUPERMARKETS CARRY THEM TOO, DEPENDING ON WHERE YOU LIVE AND HOW MUCH DEMAND THERE IS.

(continued)

Add the stock and tomato. Stir well. Season to taste with salt and pepper. Return the roast to the baking pan or skillet. Turn it in the liquid. Cover. If using a skillet, transfer the meat and vegetables to a large roasting pan and cover.

Roast for $1^1/_2$ hours. Add the vegetables to the pan. Continue to cook for 30 to 45 minutes, or until the meat is tender and cooked through so that it's easy to remove from the bone.

Remove the meat from the pan. Let it rest for about 30 minutes. Slice the meat. Serve with the vegetables and pan juices spooned over it.

OUR MEAT HABIT

Primal meat cuts (i.e., steaks, tenderloins, and prime roasts) represent only about 15 percent of the animal. To meet the intense demand for these cuts, we have created animal factories to keep up with orders for steak, steak, and more steak. If Americans changed their eating habits just a little and ate pot roast and meat loaf more often, the demand for secondary cuts—brisket, shoulder, chuck, short ribs, rump roast, and blade roast, for instance—would increase. This would mean we would need to raise and slaughter far fewer animals and use more of those we do. Such a positive adjustment in demand would allow small-scale producers to steward a system that is better for our health, more humane to the animals, and far better for the environment.

BRAISED SHORT RIBS
with CREAMY CHEESE GRITS

Few folks, whether they hail from the South or North, would associate grits with beef, but you need only think about how osso buco tastes with polenta to realize this pairing makes sense.

Italian cooks have the Native Americans to thank for polenta. Corn was imported to Europe from the New World, and when the rest of Europe was feeding the grain to livestock, the Italians were experimenting with what was to become polenta. And blowing people's minds.

Beef short ribs are the perfect braising meat to take full advantage of the rewarding union between rich meats and corn. Rich-flavored beef and horseradish is yet another discreet example of a made-to-be culinary marriage. If you have time, make this dish a day ahead and reheat gently for the very best flavor and texture.

Serves 8

¼ CUP SEA SALT

¼ CUP RAW SUGAR

2 TABLESPOONS FINELY GRATED LEMON ZEST

2 TABLESPOONS THINLY SLICED FRESH TARRAGON

2 TABLESPOONS FRESH THYME

I TEASPOON CRUSHED DRIED RED-PEPPER FLAKES

2 TEASPOONS FRESHLY GROUND BLACK PEPPER

8 POUNDS BONE-IN BEEF SHORT RIBS, TRIMMED (ABOUT I6 PIECES)

¼ CUP GRAPESEED OIL

4 LARGE CARROTS, PEELED AND CUT INTO 2"-THICK PIECES

2 CUPS PEARL OR CIPPOLINE ONIONS, PEELED

I LARGE LEEK, TRIMMED AND CUT INTO ½"-THICK SLICES

½ CUP PEELED, FINELY DICED FRESH HORSERADISH ROOT

6 GARLIC CLOVES, SMASHED

½ CUP CANNED TOMATOES

2½ CUPS RICH RED WINE, SUCH AS SYRAH, GIGONDAS AC (CÔTES DU RHONE), OR CABERNET SAUVIGNON

I CUP RICH BEEF STOCK, PREFERABLY HOMEMADE

ABOUT I5 FRESH THYME SPRIGS

I FRESH BAY LEAF

CREAMY CHEESE GRITS (PAGE 20I)

½ CUP FRESH HERBS SUCH AS YOUNG CARROT TOPS OR FLAT-LEAF PARSLEY, FOR GARNISH

(continued)

Grind the salt, sugar, lemon zest, tarragon, thyme, pepper flakes, and black pepper with a pestle in a large mortar.

Rub the ribs with a clean, dry kitchen towel. Rub the spice mixture into the meat parts of the ribs. Cover well and refrigerate overnight and up to 24 hours.

Remove the ribs from the refrigerator and wipe very dry with a clean kitchen towel or paper towels. If they are not dry, the sugar could burn when you cook the ribs. Allow to come to room temperature.

Put the oven rack in the upper-middle position of the oven. Preheat the oven to 300°F.

Heat 1 tablespoon of the oil in a heavy roasting pan or stockpot over medium-high heat. Brown the ribs, several at a time, for about 6 minutes, or until well browned. Brown every part of the ribs that can make contact with the bottom of the pan, adding the remaining oil as needed. Take care that the pan does not get so hot that the oil and beef fat scorch. Transfer the browned ribs to a holding platter.

Reduce the heat to medium and add the carrots, onions, leek, horseradish, and garlic to the pan. Cover. Cook, stirring once or twice, for about 15 minutes, or until softened and lightly browned. Use a slotted spoon to transfer the vegetables to a holding plate or bowl.

Add the tomatoes and their juices to the pan. Cook, stirring continually until the juice evaporates. As you stir, chop the tomatoes with the spoon into small pieces and let them brown a little. Add the wine. Increase the heat to medium-high. Simmer for 6 to 8 minutes, constantly scraping the browned bits from the bottom and sides of the pan with a wooden spoon, until the wine reduces by half. Add the stock, reserved vegetables, thyme, and bay leaf. Add the beef ribs and any accumulated juices. Bring to a brisk simmer over medium-high heat.

Cover tightly and roast for 2 to $2^{1}/_{2}$ hours, turning the ribs 2 or 3 times. Remove from the heat and let the ribs, vegetables, and liquid cool to room temperature in the pot.

Remove the ribs from the pot, being careful to gently push any clinging vegetables or sauce back into the pan. Skim any fat off the sauce. Let the ribs cool. Remove the meat from the bones. Trim the meat into serving-size pieces. Spread on a baking sheet or in a shallow pan.

If the meat has cooled too much, heat the oven to 350°F. Heat the meat until hot all the way through. Bring the cooking liquid and vegetables in the pot to a simmer over medium-high heat.

Spoon a mound of grits in the center of each of 8 warmed plates. Make an indentation in the center of the grits. Spoon the vegetables and sauce over the grits. Top with the trimmed ribs. Sprinkle with herbs and serve.

SHREDDED BEEF CHILI

What better way to encourage readers to use secondary cuts of meat than to make chili? I turn to brisket for this, which is full-flavored and relatively inexpensive. Everyone loves chili, and it's great for impromptu parties and family meals alike. Plus it freezes well.

Serves 8 to 10

I (4–5-POUND) BEEF BRISKET, QUARTERED FOR EASE
  OF HANDLING

SEA SALT AND FRESHLY GROUND BLACK PEPPER

4 FRESH POBLANO CHILE PEPPERS, STEMMED

¼ CUP GRAPESEED OIL

4 GARLIC CLOVES

I LARGE ONION, DICED

I TEASPOON CORIANDER SEEDS

½ TEASPOON CUMIN SEEDS

1½ CUPS CANNED TOMATOES, CHOPPED BUT NOT DRAINED

1½ CUPS SAVORY VEGETABLE STOCK (PAGE 20) OR HIGH-QUALITY
  COMMERCIAL VEGETABLE BROTH

I CANELLA OR CINNAMON STICK, ABOUT 3" LONG

I SEEDED AND SLICED SERRANO OR JALAPEÑO CHILE PEPPER
  (OPTIONAL, WEAR PLASTIC GLOVES WHEN HANDLING)

2 CUPS SLICED FRESH CILANTRO + MORE FOR GARNISH

3 CUPS COOKED DRIED HEIRLOOM BEANS (PAGE 8), WARMED

GRATED MELTING CHEESE, SUCH AS MANCHEGO, GOUDA,
  PROVOLONE, OR FONTINA (OPTIONAL)

SOUR CREAM (OPTIONAL)

Season the brisket pieces generously with salt and pepper. Set aside for 50 to 60 minutes to reach room temperature.

Cut the poblano chile peppers in half lengthwise. Scrape out the seeds. Put the peppers in a small bowl and sprinkle with salt. Pour enough hot water over the peppers to cover by about 1". Let them soak for about 30 minutes. Drain well.

Preheat the oven to 300°F.

Heat a large stockpot over medium-high heat. When hot, pour the oil into the pan. Sear the brisket, 1 piece at a time, for 8 to 10 minutes for each piece, or until nicely browned. Transfer the brisket pieces to a platter.

Smash the garlic cloves with the side of a chef's knife. Remove and discard the skins. Sprinkle the cloves with salt. Gently mash the salt into the garlic with the side of the knife.

Add the onion, coriander seeds, and cumin seeds to the pan. Cook for 4 to 5 minutes, or until the onion is translucent and lightly browned and the spices are fragrant. Reduce the heat to medium. Add the salted garlic and cook, stirring, for about 1 minute, taking care not to burn the garlic.

Stir in the tomatoes and any collected juices, the drained poblano chile peppers, and the stock and canella stick. Bring the sauce to a simmer over medium-high heat. Return the beef to the pan with any meat juices that have collected on the platter. Adjust the seasoning with salt and pepper. If you like a little heat, add the serrano or jalapeño chile pepper.

Transfer the contents of the pot to a large roasting pan. Cover the pan tightly. Braise for about 3 hours, turning over the meat pieces once during cooking. At this point, the meat should be cooked through and very tender.

Allow the meat to cool in the braising liquid just until cool enough to handle. Remove the brisket pieces, being careful to leave behind all the delicious little pieces of braised meat in the pan. Set the large pieces of meat aside. Let the contents of the pan cool. Remove and discard the canella stick.

When the contents in the pan are cool enough, transfer the liquid and vegetable chunks to the bowl of a food processor fitted with the metal blade. Pulse until nearly smooth but still with a little texture. You will need to work in batches. Or process the sauce in the pan using an immersion blender. Return the sauce to the pan. You will have about 5 cups.

Shred the beef using two forks or your fingers (or both). Return to the pan. Set over medium-low heat. Add the cilantro and cooked beans. Add some of the cooking liquid from the beans, if necessary, to keep the sauce "saucelike." Stir well while heating through. When hot and bubbling, remove from the heat and serve.

If desired, pass the cheese, sour cream, and cilantro at the table, and let people help themselves.

LEG OF PASTURE-RAISED LAMB STUFFED *with* CHESTNUTS *and* DRIED CRANBERRIES

Don't think only about mint when you roast a leg of lamb. Lamb loves other tangy flavors, too, such as the cranberries I serve with it here. Lamb also likes sweet chestnuts, which have an unctuousness that is emphasized when they absorb the delicious fats that seep from the meat. Neither the cranberries nor the chestnuts complete the lamb on their own, but when paired, this is a treat to savor.

Serves 8

STUFFING

½ CUP PORT WINE

½ CUP DRIED CRANBERRIES

2 CUPS COARSELY CHOPPED ROASTED CHESTNUTS (SEE NOTE)

4 SLICES STALE HIGH-QUALITY BREAD, CUT INTO ½" CUBES (ABOUT 2 CUPS)

3 TABLESPOONS CHOPPED FRESH HERBS, SUCH AS THYME AND SAGE

ABOUT ½ CUP BEEF, CHICKEN, OR VEGETABLE STOCK

LAMB

1 (5–5½-POUND) BONELESS LEG OF LAMB

⅓ CUP FRESH MARJORAM

¼ CUP FRESH THYME

5–6 GARLIC CLOVES, SMASHED (ABOUT 2 TABLESPOONS)

KOSHER SALT AND FRESHLY GROUND BLACK PEPPER

To prepare the stuffing: Combine the port and cranberries in a large bowl. Set aside for about 2 hours, or until the cranberries soften. Drain and discard the port, leaving the cranberries in the bowl.

Add the chestnuts, bread cubes, herbs, and enough stock to moisten the mixture. It should take on the consistency of a bread stuffing. Set aside.

To cook the lamb: Lay the lamb on the counter, boned side up. Spread the stuffing over the meat to within a few inches of the edges. Roll the lamb and tie with kitchen twine in several places to hold it together.

(continued)

Grind or process the marjoram, thyme, garlic, and salt and pepper in a mortar with a pestle or small food processor until roughly mashed. Rub this paste over the outside of the lamb. Refrigerate the lamb for at least 2 hours and up to 8 hours.

Preheat the oven to 375°F.

Let the lamb sit on a rack in a roasting pan for 20 to 30 minutes to come to room temperature. Roast the lamb for 15 to 18 minutes per pound, about $1\frac{1}{4}$ to $1\frac{1}{2}$ hours, or until an instant-read thermometer registers 130°F for medium-rare when inserted into the center of the meat. Make sure to put the thermometer into the meat, not the stuffing. If you prefer your lamb medium, roast until the thermometer registers 140°F.

Remove the lamb from the oven. Let it rest for 15 minutes before carving.

Note: YOU CAN BUY IMPORTED ROASTED CHESTNUTS, WHICH ARE SOLD IN JARS OR IN VACUUM PACKS. BE SURE TO BUY DRY CHESTNUTS, NOT THOSE PACKED IN SYRUP. YOU CAN ALSO ROAST THEM YOURSELF.

LAMB *and* WHOLE GRAIN STEW

This recipe brings out the very best that long-cooked lamb has to offer: deep, rich, earthy flavor; silken texture; and such redolent, comforting aromas that your neighbors will be driven mad—or will knock on your front door with plate in hand!

Lamb, like beef, suffers because most people care only about the prime cuts, such as racks and loin chops. The high-end restaurants that offer lamb on their menus usually sell only these cuts, so lamb, like beef, is too often raised in confined spaces to maximize the efficiency of harvesting these tender cuts. In fact, properly cooked secondary cuts, such as the shoulder I use here, are more tender and full-flavored than a medium-rare loin or rack chop.

Small farmers like to raise lamb for the diversity of its products: milk, cheese, and wool are every bit as good as the meat. Susan Sankow, who owns Beaver Brook Farm in Connecticut, offers milk, tangy artisan cheese, carded wool for knitting, and gorgeous sweaters, hats, and gloves as well as delicious meat at our farmers' markets. The crowds in front of her table are testimony to how wonderful lamb is.

Serves 6 to 8

6 CUPS SAVORY VEGETABLE STOCK (PAGE 20) OR HIGH-QUALITY
   COMMERCIAL VEGETABLE BROTH

1 CUP BLACK BARLEY

1 CUP UNCOOKED FARRO

SEA SALT AND FRESHLY GROUND BLACK PEPPER

4 POUNDS BONELESS LAMB SHOULDER MEAT, WELL TRIMMED
   AND CUT INTO 2" PIECES

4 GARLIC CLOVES, BROKEN OR SMASHED INTO CHUNKS

4 TEASPOONS + 1 TABLESPOON FINELY GRATED LEMON ZEST

¾ CUP COARSELY CHOPPED FLAT-LEAF PARSLEY

¼ CUP FRESH THYME

¼ CUP GRAPESEED OIL

1 LARGE ONION, DICED

2 LARGE LEEKS, TRIMMED AND VERY THINLY SLICED

1 FENNEL BULB, TRIMMED AND THINLY SLICED

½ CUP CHOPPED FRESH HERBS, SUCH AS THYME, SAVORY,
   MARJORAM, MINT, PARSLEY, AND TARRAGON

(continued)

Heat 3 cups of the stock in each of 2 medium stockpots. Bring both to a rapid simmer over medium-high heat. Add the barley to one pot and the farro to the other. Let the liquid come to a boil. Reduce the heat to medium, cover, and cook the grains for about 45 minutes. Check each pot after 30 minutes to ensure that the grains are not overcooking. They should still be slightly firm but palatable. Season both to taste with salt and pepper. Let them simmer for 5 to 7 minutes longer.

Drain the grains through a large strainer over a large bowl to capture the cooking liquid. There should be 2 to 3 cups of leftover cooking liquid. You will need to begin with 2 cups for the recipe. Set the cooking liquid aside. Spread the grains in a shallow pan or on a baking sheet to cool.

Meanwhile, season the lamb generously with salt and pepper. Let it stand for 50 to 60 minutes to reach room temperature.

Grind the garlic, 4 teaspoons of the lemon zest (reserve the remaining tablespoon for finishing the stew), parsley, and thyme with a pestle in a large mortar. Add about 1 teaspoon of salt. Keep grinding until the ingredients are blended but not smooth and are very aromatic. Alternatively, you can make this mixture in a small food processor.

Heat a third of the oil in a very large, heavy pot over medium-high heat. When hot, cook about a third of the lamb in the oil for 5 to 6 minutes, or until nicely browned. Transfer the lamb to a warm platter. Repeat with the remaining oil and lamb. When all the meat is browned, set aside. You will have to do this in 2 or 3 batches.

Add the onion, leeks, and fennel to the same pot. Cook for about 8 minutes, or until softened. Stir in the garlic-herb mash. Return the lamb and any accumulated juices to the pan.

Add 2 cups of the reserved grain-cooking stock. Bring the stew to a boil. Reduce the heat to medium-low, cover tightly, and simmer gently for about $1\frac{1}{2}$ hours, or until the lamb is tender. Check the stew every 20 minutes or so to see if it is necessary to add more liquid. If so, add more reserved vegetable stock or water.

To serve, gently stir the grains into the stew, along with the fresh herbs and the remaining 1 tablespoon of lemon zest.

SWEET PEA
and LEMON-RICOTTA RAVIOLI

Working with full sheets of pasta is fun—and impressive. These ravioli are far easier to make than others, because all you do is cook the pasta sheets and then fold them around the filling. The filling bursts with the fresh spring flavor of peas, and you could add spring mushrooms, early carrots, and radishes to the mix, too. I like to serve this with a sautéed garnish, like this mix of mushrooms, snow peas, and corn cooked in a little olive oil.

Serves 4 to 6

SWEET PEA SAUCE

1 QUART HEAVY CREAM

2 CUPS SHELLED PEAS (YOU CAN USE THAWED FROZEN PEAS
  IF YOU DO NOT HAVE FRESH)

KOSHER SALT AND FRESHLY GROUND BLACK PEPPER

RAVIOLI

10–12 FRESH PASTA SHEETS

1 POUND FRESH RICOTTA

1/2 CUP GRATED PARMESAN CHEESE

1 TABLESPOON OLIVE OIL

1/2 TABLESPOON KOSHER SALT

1/2 TABLESPOON FRESHLY GROUND BLACK PEPPER

GRATED ZEST OF 1 LEMON

To make the sauce: Bring the cream to a simmer in a heavy saucepan over medium heat. Lower the heat to medium-low and simmer, uncovered, for about 50 minutes, or until reduced to 2 cups. Add the peas and stir.

Transfer the sauce to a blender and puree until smooth. Strain the sauce through a fine-mesh sieve. Season the strained sauce with salt and pepper. Set aside, covered, to keep warm. You will have a little more than 2 cups of strained sauce.

To make the ravioli: Roll the pasta sheets through the rollers of a pasta machine, or roll them with a rolling pin so that they are about 1/4" thick. Trim the sheets so that they are 10" × 10". Cover with a well-wrung kitchen towel.

(continued)

Mix together the ricotta, Parmesan, oil, salt, pepper, and lemon zest in a saucepan. Heat over medium heat, stirring constantly, for 1 to 2 minutes, or until blended and warmed through.

Bring about 2" of water to a boil in a wide, deep skillet or similar pan. Simmer a few pasta sheets at a time for 1 to 2 minutes, or until al dente. Lift the sheets from the water with a slotted spoon and drain in a colander. Lay the sheets on a flat surface with a little water clinging to them so that they don't stick together.

Lay a pasta sheet on a work surface. Scoop about 2 tablespoons of the filling directly onto the center. Fold the pasta over the filling like an envelope: Fold the top of the sheet over the filling, then fold the bottom of the sheet about two-thirds over the top fold. Fold the sides in to form a square ravioli.

Spoon the sauce onto 6 warm plates and top with a ravioli. Garnish with sautéed seasonal vegetables and fresh herbs, if desired.

MACARONI *and* CHEESE

My mom knew how much we loved her macaroni and cheese, and she leveraged that fondness to get us to do just about anything, from mowing the lawn to peeling a couple of bushels of apples during canning season. The dish was an indulgence for us because of the expense of cream. One of our chores was bringing in the milk left by the milkman and storing it in the refrigerator. I remember how excited we would be when we spied a small bottle of cream in with the milk. Macaroni and cheese day!

Mom always added extra protein to the casserole in the form of pork belly or bacon. Although the rest of the family liked bacon the best, Mom and I preferred the pork belly, agreeing that the flavor of good cream and mild cheese were best richened with the meatiness and fat of the pork belly. To us, the smokiness of the bacon detracted from these just a little.

Serves 6

6 CUPS HEAVY CREAM

SEA SALT

1 POUND GOOD-QUALITY SEMOLINA OR SEMOLINA/LEGUME-BASED SHORT, CHUNKY PASTA, SUCH AS PENNE OR ZITI

2 TABLESPOONS GRAPESEED OIL

1/2 POUND CURED, BRAISED PORK BELLY OR THICK-CUT BACON, CUT INTO 1/3"–1/2" CUBES

2 CUPS GRATED MELTING CHEESE, SUCH AS GOUDA (I LIKE CYPRESS GROVE MIDNIGHT MOON, A DOMESTIC GOAT CHEESE GOUDA) OR PECORINO ROMANO, OR A MIXTURE OF THE TWO

3 TABLESPOONS FRESH THYME

2 TABLESPOONS UNSALTED BUTTER

FRESHLY GROUND BLACK PEPPER

1 CUP FRESH BREAD CRUMBS

Bring the cream to a rapid simmer in a large saucepan over medium-high heat. Reduce the heat to medium-low. Simmer gently for 50 to 60 minutes, or until the cream reduces by half, to about 3 cups. Cover and set aside to keep warm.

Fill a large pot with about 1½ gallons of water. Add enough salt so that the water tastes like seawater. Bring to a boil over high heat. Add the pasta. Cook for 8 to 10 minutes, or just until al dente. Drain well by tossing in a large colander. This kind of pasta holds a lot of water in its nooks and crannies. Spread the drained pasta on a baking sheet to dry slightly.

Preheat the oven to 350°F.

Meanwhile, heat a heavy skillet over medium heat. When hot, pour the oil into the pan. Add the pork belly. Cook for about 5 minutes, or until lightly browned but still tender in the center. Do not cook until fully crisp (unless you really like crispy foods). With a slotted spoon, transfer the pork belly to a plate lined with a kitchen towel to drain. Discard all but 2 tablespoons of the fat in the pan.

Bring the reduced cream to a gentle simmer. Stir in 1¾ cups of the cheese, followed by the thyme. Stir in the butter. Season to taste with salt and pepper. Taste before you season; the cheese is salty, so you may not need any salt.

Toss the pasta with the cheese sauce and pork belly in a large bowl. If the mixture is too stiff, thin the sauce with a little milk or cream. Transfer to a baking dish large enough to hold the pasta.

Toss the bread crumbs with the reserved fat and the remaining ¼ cup of cheese. Sprinkle the crumbs over the baking dish.

Bake for 15 to 20 minutes, or until the pasta is bubbling nicely and the top is crisp and browned.

Chapter 6

SIDE DISHES

A wholesome meal should include a protein, starch, and vegetable. When this combination is oversimplified, it can compromise our health. In contemporary cooking, we've simplified the starch to white potatoes, instant rice, or frozen dinner rolls, which only contribute to our waistlines. We used to celebrate our cereal crops by adding them to soups, stews, and porridges and baking wholesome breads. These grains provided sustenance and awesome nutrients and acted as delicious alternatives or meal stretchers to the expensive protein.

Vegetables (and fruit) represent a perfect marriage between man and nature. Our nutritional needs and what nature provides are so perfectly in sync that if we ate as many vegetables as we should, there would be no need for otherwise healthy folks to down vitamin supplements.

Even better, eating vegetables and fruits remains one of the tastiest ways to enjoy the seasons. While long gone are the days when young lamb was eaten only in the spring and fresh pork in the late fall, asparagus still is most tender in the spring, corn and tomatoes are best in the summer, apples are at their peak in the autumn, and winter squash is finest in the cold months. These are the facts.

Enter the convenience age, when the cheapest foods are the most highly processed and the foods that are best for us are the most expensive. Our dinner plates suffer, and because we are not as active as we were when we, as a society, ate more seasonally, we suffer. And yet, food companies have tried to bend nature to their will with only limited success. For many of us, it's been hard to forgo the idea of really good BLTs in the winter, but I believe that we are once again embracing the idea of eating seasonally, this time by choice rather than by necessity. It's an exciting, productive, rewarding, and delicious way to take charge of our health and the health of the environment.

How do we accomplish this? By buying and eating more whole grains and vegetables, of course! I encourage you not to think of the plate as having separate components—like the old-fashioned cafeteria plates with ridges meant to keep the meat from touching the vegetables—but to understand that the grains or vegetables can be part of the protein dish and vice versa. Also, we should put less reliance on protein and white starches. Not only will we be healthier, we also will enjoy our food more and save money.

GRILLED CORN ON THE COB

ROASTED HEIRLOOM SQUASH
WITH SEA SALT AND LOCAL HONEY

BLACK BARLEY AND AUTUMN VEGETABLES

RISOTTO-STYLE SUMMER HEIRLOOM FARRO

BUTTER AND CHEESE HOMINY

CREAMY CHEESE GRITS

SCALLOPED ROOT VEGETABLES

WHOLE ROASTED WINTER SQUASH

CELERY ROOT PUREE

HEIRLOOM MASHED POTATOES

PAN-WILTED KALE WITH PEAR
AND CURED BERKSHIRE PORK BELLY

COLLARD GREENS

SPICY HONEY-ROASTED CAULIFLOWER

BRUSSELS SPROUTS WITH DRIED CRANBERRIES

FRESH HEIRLOOM BEANS

SAUTÉED MUSHROOMS WITH CARAMELIZED SHALLOTS
AND PORK BELLY

APPLE-ROSEMARY PUREE

SPICY EGGPLANT

PEACH AND FENNEL SLAW

APPLE SLAW

GRILLED CORN *on* THE COB

Caution: The recipe you are about to read may seem like a pain in the tuchus, but I would never go through this rigmarole unless it was truly rewarding—and it is! You have to peel the green leaves from the corn and remove as much of the silk as you can, and then return the leaves to their original position. I stuff the husks with ingredients that flavor the corn as it grills.

Serves 4

8 EARS VERY FRESH SWEET CORN

⅔ CUP ROASTED GARLIC CLOVES (ABOUT 1 HEAD OF GARLIC)

¼ CUP FINELY SLICED FRESH CILANTRO (ABOUT ¼ OF A BUNCH OR ½ OUNCE)

¼ CUP FINELY SLICED FRESH CHERVIL OR TARRAGON

1 TABLESPOON FRESHLY GRATED LEMON ZEST

¼ CUP UNSALTED BUTTER, SOFTENED

SEA SALT AND FRESHLY GROUND BLACK PEPPER

Put the unhusked ears of corn in 1 or 2 pots or bowls. Cover with cold water. Let the ears soak for about 1 hour.

Cut kitchen string into sixteen 12" lengths. Soak the string in cold water.

Prepare a charcoal or wood grill for indirect grilling. The cool part of the grill should be large enough to accommodate all the ears. Let the coals reach their peak and begin to cool.

Meanwhile, smash the roasted garlic, cilantro, chervil, and lemon zest with a pestle in a mortar. Work in the butter and season to taste with salt and pepper. Do not let the mixture get too fine. It should retain texture, and pieces of garlic and herbs should be visible. You will have about ⅔ cup of herb paste.

Peel back the corn husks, one leaf at a time, until the silk is exposed. Remove the silks. Rub each ear with generous amounts of the herb paste. Fold the leaves back over the seasoned cobs in as close to the original order as you can. Tie a kitchen string around the top where the leaves join and overlap to secure the husks. Tie a second piece of string midway down the ear. Trim any excess string.

Lay the ears of corn on the cool side of the grill. Cook for about 12 minutes, turning continually, until all sides of the corn are lightly browned and hot. If one side of the ears chars, it's okay (my wife, Lori, prefers this).

Move the corn to the hotter part of the grill over the coals. Cook for about 5 minutes longer, or until the strings burn off and the husks begin to char.

Transfer the corn to a platter large enough to hold them—and stand back!

ROASTED HEIRLOOM SQUASH *with* SEA SALT *and* LOCAL HONEY

Squash takes just about any kind of heat. When you cook it as I do here, the flesh dehydrates a little and turns meaty, so all it needs is a little drizzle of honey and a sprinkle of salt. Squash is forgiving no matter how you cook it, but only if you start with a good specimen. If you prefer, cook it to the texture you like best, and don't follow a prescribed time.

Serves 6 to 8

- 4–5 POUNDS HARD WINTER SQUASH IN 2 VARIETIES, SUCH AS BUTTERNUT AND KABOCHA, SEEDED (BUT NOT PEELED) AND CUT INTO 1" SLICES OR WEDGES, WHICHEVER SHAPE BEST REPRESENTS THE ORIGINAL SHAPE OF THE SQUASH
- 2 TABLESPOONS LOCAL HONEY
- ¼ CUP EXTRA-VIRGIN OLIVE OIL
- SEA SALT AND FRESHLY GROUND BLACK PEPPER
- 2–3 TABLESPOONS CHOPPED FRESH HERBS, SUCH AS SAGE, ROSEMARY, THYME, OREGANO, AND MARJORAM

Preheat the oven to 375°F.

Lightly drizzle the squash with the honey and oil in a large bowl. Using your fingers, rub the honey and oil into the squash pieces to distribute evenly. Sprinkle with salt and pepper. Arrange the squash pieces, skin side down, on a baking sheet.

Bake the squash for 35 to 45 minutes, turning the pieces once or twice during cooking, or until the squash is fork-tender when pierced with a fork or a small, sharp knife.

Transfer the squash to a serving platter or bowl. Sprinkle with the fresh herbs, a little more honey, and a little sea salt. Serve hot.

BLACK BARLEY
and AUTUMN VEGETABLES

As you have no doubt figured out before now, I am a huge fan of ancient and underused grains, such as quinoa and black barley. This is one of my favorite ways to serve black barley—cooked pilaf-style—but I like it other ways too. If you are in the mood for a wholesome, hearty, and full-flavored fall dish, you have hit pay dirt with this recipe! For the best texture, start the day before and soak the grain for a full 24 hours, but if you have time for only 3 or 4 hours of soaking, you won't be disappointed.

Serves 4 to 6

8 OUNCES UNCOOKED BLACK BARLEY

1 SMALL BUNCH FRESH THYME

2 BAY LEAVES

¼ TEASPOON BLACK PEPPERCORNS

GRATED ZEST OF 1 ORANGE

¼ CUP DICED PARSNIP (1 SMALL PARSNIP)

¼ CUP DICED CARROT (1 SMALL CARROT)

¼ CUP DICED CELERY ROOT (1 SMALL ROOT)

1 TABLESPOON UNSALTED BUTTER

KOSHER SALT AND FRESHLY GROUND BLACK PEPPER

FLAT-LEAF PARSLEY LEAVES, FOR GARNISH

Put the barley in a bowl. Pour enough cold water over it to cover by about 1". Set aside to soak for about 24 hours.

Lay an 8" × 8" double thickness of cheesecloth on a work surface. Pile the thyme, bay leaves, peppercorns, and orange zest in the center of the cheesecloth. Tie the corners together to make a bouquet garni.

Drain the barley. Transfer it to a large pot. Add 4 cups of water and the bouquet garni. Stir once or twice. Bring to a boil over medium-high heat. Reduce the heat to medium-low. Simmer very gently for 25 to 30 minutes, or until the barley is tender.

If necessary, drain the excess liquid from the pot. Add the parsnip, carrot, celery root, and butter. Stir to mix. Continue cooking over medium heat for 6 to 8 minutes, or until the vegetables are tender and the butter melts. Season to taste with salt and pepper, garnish with the parsley, and serve.

RISOTTO-STYLE SUMMER HEIRLOOM FARRO

Thankfully, farro, an old-world grain, made it to the new world so that we could enjoy this amazing dish. This dish resembles risotto, but, in deference to our American heritage, perhaps it should be called porridge. Semantics aside, it's a great way to use summer squash.

Serves 8

4 TABLESPOONS OLIVE OIL

1 LARGE YELLOW ONION, DICED

8 FRESH ZUCCHINI BLOSSOMS (OPTIONAL)

1 CUP UNCOOKED FARRO

4 CUPS CHICKEN STOCK, PREFERABLY HOMEMADE

1 LARGE ZUCCHINI, DICED

1½ CUPS FRESH SWEET CORN KERNELS

1 PINT CHERRY TOMATOES, HALVED

2 TABLESPOONS UNSALTED BUTTER

KOSHER SALT AND FRESHLY GROUND BLACK PEPPER

1 LEMON, SLICED

Heat 2 tablespoons of the oil in a large, deep skillet over medium-high heat. Add the onion. Cook for 4 to 5 minutes, or until softened but not browned. Add the zucchini blossoms, if using, reduce the heat to medium, and cook for about 1 minute. Remove the blossoms to a plate and keep warm. Add the farro. Cook for 2 to 3 minutes just to coat with the oil and mix with the onions.

Pour the stock into the skillet. Stir the farro and onions. Bring to a boil over medium-high heat. Reduce the heat to medium. Simmer, stirring frequently, for 40 to 45 minutes, at which time the farro should be tender and the stock evaporated. Add more stock if needed during cooking to keep the farro moist.

Heat the remaining 2 tablespoons of oil in another large skillet over medium-high heat. When hot, add the zucchini and corn kernels. Cook for 10 to 12 minutes, or until the vegetables brown. Add the tomatoes. Cook for about 1 minute to warm through. Add the farro and toss to mix. Add the butter and stir until melted. Season to taste with salt and pepper.

Spoon the farro onto each of 8 plates. Garnish each plate with a zucchini blossom.

BUTTER AND CHEESE HOMINY

Among the dishes that evoke less-than-fond memories for many is hominy, largely because hominy is so often poorly cooked. Yet, when cooked properly, whole hominy, like grits, is among the most comforting of foods.

We are wired to like the flavor of corn (think corn chips and corn tortillas), and now that it's possible to get whole hominy, thanks to Glen Roberts at Anson Mills and the late John Mohawk of Iroquois White Corn Project in upstate New York, every home cook should try it. It's simple, though not quick.

First, hominy must be soaked and then cooked for a long time. As it cooks, the dried corn "blooms" as the flesh emerges and the corn resembles wet popcorn. It is actually the expansion of the protein and starches that creates the look of cooked hominy. Some kernels may remain intact, which is fine, so long as you achieve moist, meaty nuggets of corn with a classic corn chip flavor. The flavor lends itself extremely well to butter and cheese.

Serves 6

3 CUPS WHOLE HOMINY (WWW.ANSONMILLS.COM)

1/2 TABLESPOON BAKING SODA

1/4–1/2 CUP UNSALTED BUTTER, AT ROOM TEMPERATURE

1/4–1/2 CUP GRATED MELTING CHEESE, SUCH AS MILD CHEDDAR OR ROMANO

1/4 CUP SLICED SHALLOTS

1/4 CUP CHOPPED FRESH HERBS, SUCH AS THYME, SAVORY, AND PARSLEY

1 TABLESPOON GRAPESEED OIL

KOSHER SALT AND FRESHLY GROUND BLACK PEPPER

Soak the hominy in water to cover mixed with the baking soda in a large bowl for 24 hours. Stir the hominy 2 or 3 times during soaking. Remove any skins that float to the top. Drain the hominy in a colander and rinse very well.

Bring the hominy and 6 cups of water to a simmer in a pot over medium-high heat. Reduce the heat to low. Simmer, partially covered, for 3 to 4 hours, or until the hominy is tender and blooms so that it resembles wet popcorn.

Drain the hominy well. Return it to the pot. Add the butter, cheese, shallots, and herbs. Stir well. Finish with the oil. Season to taste with salt and pepper.

CREAMY CHEESE GRITS

Most people reach for instant grits when they cook grits. Shame on them! Anyone who has had real, honest-to-goodness grits never minds waiting an additional 30 to 40 minutes for the genuine article. In this recipe, I start with really good grits and cook them even longer than normal.

For them to be good, though, you must start with great grits and then cook them with care. Grits are not something you can put on the stove and walk away from; you have to stir them often. It's not that you can't tend to other kitchen tasks, but the grits need and deserve almost continual attention. When you cook them, watch closely for "first starch." This is when the more finely ground grits actually begin to thicken the cooking liquid and almost look like they are suspended in milk or cream. Stir grits regularly until they achieve first starch, then let them simmer at the lowest possible heat for however long it takes to finish cooking. Properly cooked grits are almost soufflélike when they reach first starch. They are so fluffy, you may feel you don't even need the cheese, although it's delicious. If you omit the cheese, a few pats of butter stirred into the grits does the trick.

Serves 4

- 1 cup yellow hominy grits (I like Antebellum grits from Anson Mills)
- 2 teaspoons sea salt
- 1 cup milk
- ¼ cup grated aged goat cheese or sheep's milk cheese, such as Cypress Grove Midnight Moon or Pecorino Romano
- Salt and freshly ground black pepper

Soak the grits in about 2½ cups of water in a mixing bowl overnight or up to 24 hours.

Drain well. Transfer the grits to a pot. Add water to cover by about 1". Add the salt.

Bring the grits to a gentle simmer over medium heat. Cover. Cook on medium-low heat for about 1 hour, or until the grits are tender and quite thick. Stir the grits a few times during cooking so that they don't stick to the bottom of the pan.

Add the milk and cheese. Stir until creamy. Season to taste with salt and pepper and serve.

SCALLOPED
ROOT VEGETABLES

Everybody who has tasted scalloped potatoes at their finest loves them, but unfortunately, insipid versions litter the landscape, from the just-add-water variety to the over- or undercooked samples ladled onto plates in school, hospital, and college cafeterias. What a shame, as scalloped potatoes is truly a great American dish.

I choose to use other root vegetables for this dish, in part because so many potatoes are modified to the point where they are nothing more than simple carbohydrates with a mealy texture and little flavor. This recipe provides the creamy, crusty, dairy-flavored goodness of the best scalloped potatoes, enhanced by the broad flavor spectrum contributed by the rutabaga, sweet potatoes, turnips, and celery root. If there is a drawback to this, it's the investment of time, from reducing the cream to slicing and then layering the vegetables. But as with all good investments, this one pays off in terms of flavor, texture, and even cooking. One of the secrets is to slice the vegetables evenly and layer them carefully. Finally, this recipe can easily be doubled for a crowd.

Serves 8

3 CUPS HEAVY CREAM

½ RUTABAGA, PEELED AND VERY THINLY SLICED

I LARGE SWEET POTATO, PEELED AND VERY THINLY SLICED

I SMALL CELERY ROOT, PEELED AND VERY THINLY SLICED

I–2 TURNIPS, PEELED AND VERY THINLY SLICED

SEA SALT AND FRESHLY GROUND BLACK PEPPER

⅓ CUP CHOPPED FRESH HERBS, SUCH AS THYME, CHERVIL,
    ROSEMARY, OR FLAT-LEAF PARSLEY

I ONION, VERY THINLY SLICED

Bring the cream to a rapid simmer in a heavy saucepan over medium-high heat. Reduce the heat. Simmer gently for 30 to 35 minutes, or until reduced to about $1\frac{1}{2}$ cups. Cover to keep warm.

Preheat the oven to 375°.

Rub a little grapeseed oil over the bottom and up the sides of a baking dish that measures about 12" × 9" and is about 2" deep. Shingle the rutabaga slices in the dish, overlapping each by about 1", until the bottom of the dish is fully covered with a single layer. Repeat with the sweet potato, celery root, and turnips. Sprinkle the turnips liberally with salt and pepper and about a third of the chopped herbs. Spread half of the onion over the turnips, being careful that it is evenly distributed.

(continued)

Drizzle a third of the warm, reduced cream over the vegetables.

Repeat the layering process. Add another third of the cream.

Finish with a layer of rutabaga and sweet potato. Reserve the remaining cream and herbs. If you have leftover vegetables, arrange them decoratively over the top.

Cover the baking dish tightly with foil. Bake for about 40 minutes. Uncover the baking dish and carefully tip it to drain the excess liquid into a small saucepan. There will be 3 to 4 tablespoons of liquid.

Drizzle the top of the casserole with the remaining cream. Return to the oven, uncovered, for 15 to 20 minutes longer.

In the meantime, put the saucepan holding the drained liquid over medium-high heat. Bring to a boil. Cook for 3 to 4 minutes, or until slightly reduced and thickened. Drizzle the sauce over the casserole during the final few minutes of cooking. (If you can't get around to this last step or if it seems too fussy for your style, no worries! The scalloped vegetables still will be delicious.)

Remove the casserole from the oven. Sprinkle the remaining third of the herbs over the top and serve.

Note: IF YOU ARE NOT READY TO SERVE THE SCALLOPED VEGETABLES RIGHT AWAY, LET THEM COOL COMPLETELY IN THE DISH. AFTER RUNNING A KNIFE AROUND THE EDGES, UPEND ON A CUTTING BOARD. YOU CAN CUT THE CASSEROLE INTO SECTIONS AND REHEAT LATER BY SAUTÉING THEM UNTIL BROWNED AND CRISP ON BOTH SIDES.

WHOLE ROASTED WINTER SQUASH

Here is an easy and fail-safe way to cook winter squash—with no need to wrestle with the slippery seeds and strings. When you cook the squash with the seeds still inside it, those pesky strings magically disappear and you can scoop out the seeds, which are ready for toasting. The squash is now all set for hash or soup.

Serves 4

I LARGE OR 2 SMALL HARD WINTER SQUASH (ABOUT 5 POUNDS TOTAL), SUCH AS KABOCHA, BUTTERCUP, BUTTERNUT, AND HUBBARD

I–2 TABLESPOONS GRAPESEED OR OLIVE OIL

SEA SALT AND FRESHLY GROUND BLACK PEPPER

Preheat the oven to 325°F.

Cut the squash in half with a large knife. If possible, slice it horizontally so that the most interior is exposed. If it's easier to slice the squash through its "equator," that's okay.

Rub the cut sides with enough oil to coat. Arrange the squash, cut side up, in a shallow pan. You may need to slice a sliver off the bottom of the squash to enable it to sit upright.

Roast the squash for 35 to 60 minutes, or until a small, sharp knife easily pierces the meatiest part of the flesh. Check the squash after 35 minutes. Depending on the size of the squash, it may need to cook as long as an hour.

Turn the oven temperature up to 350°F.

Remove the squash from the oven and set aside until cool enough to handle. Scoop the seeds from the cavities. They slip easily from the pulp. Set the seeds aside for toasting.

To toast the seeds, toss them with a little oil and spread on a baking sheet. Sprinkle with sea salt and toast in the oven for 15 to 25 minutes, stirring 2 or 3 times, or until lightly browned and fragrant. Alternatively, cook the seeds in a skillet coated with a few tablespoons of oil. Season with sea salt.

Peel the skin from the squash. Season with a little salt and pepper and serve with the seeds sprinkled over it. Or use the squash in a recipe calling for cooked squash. It can be refrigerated for up to a week.

CELERY ROOT PUREE

Everyone knows how versatile mashed potatoes are, but I'd like to nominate this puree as a worthy competitor. Add it to soups and stews to thicken and flavor them, thin the puree for a more saucelike consistency, or blend it with other root vegetable mashes or purees for amazing silkiness and deep flavor. On its own, I love it with pork, beef, and fish (see Pan-Roasted Blackfish, page 126). And this puree pairs very well with mushrooms and the noble truffle, that most highly revered and exorbitantly priced mushroom. Luckily, celeriac—or celery root—is dirt cheap.

Serves 4

- 2 CUPS MILK
- 1 CUP WATER
- 1 POUND CELERY ROOT, PEELED AND CUT INTO 1" DICE
- 2 TABLESPOONS UNSALTED BUTTER, SOFTENED
- 2 TEASPOONS SEA SALT
- FRESHLY GROUND BLACK PEPPER

Bring the milk, water, and celery root to a simmer in a saucepan over medium heat. Reduce the heat and cook very gently for about 30 minutes, or until the celery root is very tender. Drain and reserve the cooking liquid.

Transfer the celery root to a blender. Add the butter. Puree until smooth and the consistency of thinned mashed potatoes. Add a little of the reserved cooking liquid if necessary for the right consistency.

Season with the salt and pepper to taste and serve.

HEIRLOOM MASHED POTATOES

I can't emphasize enough how much of a difference really good heirloom potatoes make when it comes to mashed potatoes. When the potatoes are fresh and flavorful, there is no reason to add truffle oil or Parmesan cheese or caramelized onions. The potatoes themselves shine through. Wander through a farmers' market and select as many different types of potatoes as you can find. Even purple potatoes make great mashers! But, if you improvise, don't add so many other things that you mask the flavor of the potatoes. Take my advice: Whisper, don't shout.

Do not overcook the spuds, or they will be sticky and gummy. Let them dry out a little so that when you mash them they are nice and fluffy. Use a food mill or ricer rather than a processor or blender: It makes a discernible difference in the final texture of the potatoes.

Serves 4

2 POUNDS HEIRLOOM POTATOES, PEELED AND CUT INTO
  2"–3" WEDGES OR PIECES
1–2 TABLESPOONS KOSHER SALT
½ CUP WHOLE MILK
¼ CUP UNSALTED BUTTER, AT ROOM TEMPERATURE
FRESHLY GROUND BLACK PEPPER

Put the potatoes in a large saucepan with water to cover. Add enough salt so that the water tastes very lightly of salt. Bring to a simmer over high heat. Reduce the heat so that the water barely simmers. Cook for about 15 minutes, or until a knife easily pierces the potatoes.

Drain the potatoes, reserving some of the cooking water in a cup. Return the potatoes to the pot. Stir over medium heat for 1 to 2 minutes, or until the potatoes dry out.

Meanwhile, heat the milk and butter in a small saucepan until the butter melts. Season lightly with salt, so that the milk tastes a little like the sea. Add some pepper.

Transfer the potatoes to a food mill or ricer held over the empty cooking pot. Mill the potatoes into the pot.

Slowly stir in the milk and butter mixture until the potatoes reach the desired consistency. If you have added all the milk and the potatoes need more liquid, add some of the reserved cooking water from the potatoes.

PAN-WILTED KALE *with* PEAR *and* CURED BERKSHIRE PORK BELLY

Dark, leafy greens—full of good flavor and personality as well as beneficial nutrients—are great to eat all winter, but I admit that if you serve them week in and week out, you can get tired of them. The solution is to find new ways to cook them, and this is one of the best.

In this recipe, opposites attract: bitter greens and sweet pears, both enhanced by the fatty, salty pork belly. The textures are a study in opposites too: soft pears, chewy greens, and crispy pork. Can you beat it?

Serves 4

4–6 OUNCES PORK BELLY OR HIGH-QUALITY, THICK-CUT BACON, CUT INTO 1" PIECES

¼ CUP SLICED ONION

½ POUND KALE, TOUGH STEMS REMOVED, LEAVES COARSELY CUT AND RINSED WELL, WITH SOME WATER STILL CLINGING TO THE LEAVES

1 RIPE PEAR, SUCH AS BOSC OR ANJOU, STEMMED, SEEDED, AND CUT INTO 12 WEDGES

SEA SALT

Brown the pork belly in a skillet over medium heat, until crisp on the outside. Pour off most of the fat. Set the pork belly aside on a warm plate lined with paper towels.

Add the onion to the skillet. Cook, stirring often, for 1 to 2 minutes, or until soft and lightly browned.

Increase the heat to high. Add the kale. Splash with a little water. Cook, stirring constantly, for 4 to 5 minutes, or until the kale completely collapses and wilts. Stir in the pear wedges and cooked pork belly.

Remove the skillet from the heat. Cover and let it stand for 10 minutes. Season to taste with salt and serve.

COLLARD GREENS

Growing up, we had collard greens on our supper table often. Sometimes they were mixed with other greens, but collards were nearly always part of the mix. Although some folks might see this as a form of torture, others understand that collards are an important factor both in providing good health to the family and maintaining solid supper-table economics. Whenever my mom served fried chicken or smothered pork chops, the table was also laden with vegetables, beans, and grains. As food cop, Dad saw to it that we ate some of everything before we could have a piece of fried chicken or a pork chop. This meant that, depending on the meal, we had room for only one or two pieces of chicken or maybe half of a pork chop, and that was the point. Meat was expensive; collard greens were not. Fortunately, it was all delicious, so we never really minded.

Any good cook's recipe for collard greens is going to be simple, although if you under-cook them, you will be disappointed. They are not like broccoli; they should not be bright green. Classic collard greens call for ham-hock stock, but this recipe uses chicken stock as some folks prefer not to eat pork. If you love that good pork flavor, garnish the cooked greens with thick-cut bacon.

Serves 4

2 CUPS CHICKEN BROTH, PREFERABLY HOMEMADE

ABOUT 1 POUND COLLARD GREENS, STEMS REMOVED, CHOPPED
INTO 4" PIECES

1 LARGE ONION, SLICED

1 JALAPEÑO CHILE PEPPER, HALVED

1 TABLESPOON MALT OR APPLE CIDER VINEGAR

¼ TEASPOON SALT

⅛ TEASPOON FRESHLY GROUND BLACK PEPPER

4 SLICES SEARED THICK-CUT BACON (OPTIONAL)

Bring the broth to a rapid simmer in a large pot over medium-high heat. Add the greens, onion, and chile pepper. Reduce the heat to low and simmer for about 2 hours, or until the collards are very tender.

Drain. Season with the vinegar, salt, and black pepper.

SPICY HONEY-ROASTED CAULIFLOWER

I see cauliflower as a blank slate, just waiting for some culinary deftness—and yet many people seldom apply creativity to "boring vegetables" like cauliflower and broccoli. This recipe is a wonderful way to perk up cauliflower, which when left whole and roasted almost becomes a centerpiece. There is a feeling of abundance when it's set on the table and everyone says "wow!" You can mix the herbs or use only one kind, depending what is fresh at the market or in your garden.

Serves 8

2 WHOLE HEADS CAULIFLOWER, TRIMMED AND CLEANED

½ CUP FRESH BREAD CRUMBS

½ CUP LOCAL HONEY

⅓ CUP CHOPPED FRESH HERBS, SUCH AS THYME, TARRAGON, PARSLEY, AND/OR ROSEMARY

¼ CUP WHOLE GRAIN MUSTARD

¼ CUP (1 STICK) BUTTER, SOFTENED

Preheat the oven to 375°F.

Pierce the heart of each cauliflower stem with a long, slim paring knife. Put both heads, stem side down, in a deep baking dish large enough to hold them comfortably. Add about ¼" of water. Cover the pan with foil. Bake for about 30 minutes.

Remove the foil and pour off the water. Return the cauliflower to the oven. Increase the oven temperature to 400°F. Bake for about 5 minutes to dry the cauliflower.

Meanwhile, stir together the bread crumbs, honey, herbs, mustard, and butter in a small mixing bowl.

Remove the cauliflower from the oven. Coat both heads with the bread-crumb mixture. Return to the oven. Roast for about 12 minutes, or until the cauliflower heads are nicely browned and tender when pierced with a fork or small, sharp knife.

BRUSSELS SPROUTS
with DRIED CRANBERRIES

I have noticed something of a sea change when it comes to attitudes about Brussels sprouts: More folks claim to love them than hate them. I think this is because we are getting away from traditional ways of cooking them so that they are not boring or "just another type of cabbage." This is one of the best ways I know to play up their caramel-like, nutty sweetness, enhanced by the shallots and wine-sweetened cranberries.

Serves 4

1 CUP DRIED CRANBERRIES

¼ CUP SEMIDRY RIESLING WINE

4 CUPS BRUSSELS SPROUTS (ABOUT 1½ POUNDS)

2 TABLESPOONS GRAPESEED OIL

4 SHALLOTS, PEELED AND THINLY SLICED

2 TABLESPOONS UNSALTED BUTTER

KOSHER SALT AND FRESHLY GROUND PEPPER

Soak the cranberries in the wine in a small bowl for about 1 hour, giving the wine ample time to infuse the cranberries. Drain and discard any leftover wine.

Remove the outer leaves from the Brussels sprouts. Rinse them well. Do not let them dry completely, as the residual moisture helps them cook thoroughly. Halve the Brussels sprouts.

Heat the oil in a large skillet over medium-high heat until hot. Put about half of the Brussels sprouts, cut side down, in the skillet. Cook for 4 to 5 minutes, or until they brown nicely. Turn the sprouts over. Add the shallots and cook for 2 to 3 minutes, stirring occasionally, until the shallots soften. Transfer to a bowl. Cook the remaining Brussels sprouts. When these are done, return the first batch to the pan. (You may choose to cook the sprouts and shallots in 2 skillets at once, rather than in batches.)

Add the drained cranberries and the butter. Reduce the heat to low. Cover and cook for 1 to 2 minutes longer, or until the sprouts are just tender when pierced with the tip of a sharp knife. Season to taste with salt and pepper and serve.

FRESH HEIRLOOM BEANS

Few people buy fresh shell beans anymore. I love them, and those I don't grow in my garden, I buy at farmers' markets when I see them: beautiful, long, crimson-and-white pods of fresh cranberry beans; cream-colored pods of Indian woman beans; golden yellow pods of tiger's eye beans, with their black spots, like eyes; and long white pods of appaloosa beans, with black spots. Sitting outside with a pile of beans on your lap and shelling them into a bowl is a summertime joy and a task kids enjoy too.

Fresh beans take from 30 to 45 minutes to cook, depending on when they were harvested. After all, food is not a manufactured product that always behaves the same way. Those ready for picking in the summertime are more tender and cook more quickly than those picked in the fall, which are a little more mature and need close to 45 minutes to cook fully. Once you've made them a few times, you will be able to tell by feel when the beans are done. Depending on the variety and size of the beans, the weight of the bean pods you need will vary between 2 and 3 pounds.

Serves 6

3 CUPS SHELLED BEANS (2–3 POUNDS BEANS IN THEIR PODS)

5–6 FRESH THYME SPRIGS

2 GARLIC CLOVES, PEELED OR UNPEELED

½ FRESH BAY LEAF

PINCH OF BAKING SODA

SEA SALT

1–2 TABLESPOONS UNSALTED BUTTER

1–2 TEASPOONS FRESH THYME LEAVES

Put the shelled beans in a large saucepan and cover generously with water. Add the thyme sprigs, garlic, bay leaf, and baking soda. The baking soda helps to soften the beans' skin. (Do not add salt to the water; salt toughens the beans.)

Bring the water to a simmer over medium heat. Reduce the heat to low. Simmer very gently for 30 to 45 minutes, or until the beans are nice and tender.

Sprinkle enough salt into the water until the water tastes like seawater. Remove the pan from the heat. Let it stand for 15 to 20 minutes, or until the beans are perfectly salted. At this point the beans can be drained, cooled, and refrigerated for up to 5 days or used in recipes that call for cooked fresh heirloom beans.

To serve right away or when the beans have been reheated in a little water, drain the beans and serve hot-tossed with the butter and thyme.

SAUTÉED MUSHROOMS *with* CARAMELIZED SHALLOTS *and* PORK BELLY

This is one of those dishes that will haunt you when it's been too long since you've eaten it. Use any kind of mushrooms, and witness how the pork belly or bacon and caramelized shallots marry with their earthiness. You might want to add a splash of excellent vinegar or some freshly grated lemon zest, but neither is necessary.

Mushrooms are one of the best examples of how nature and man can partner to achieve soaring heights. There are so many varieties available from farmers' markets as well as supermarkets that you can experiment to your heart's content. Whenever you come across some especially appealing fresh mushrooms, go home and cook them up with some caramelized shallots. Pure bliss.

Serves 4

1 TABLESPOON GRAPESEED OIL

1 CUP CUBED (¼"–⅓") CURED PORK BELLY (PAGE 212)
  OR THICK-CUT BACON

½ CUP THINLY SLICED SHALLOTS (1–2 SHALLOTS)

4 CUPS ASSORTED MUSHROOMS, SUCH AS OYSTER, BLACK TRUMPET,
  CHANTERELLE, AND CREMINI, TRIMMED (ABOUT ½ POUND)

1 TABLESPOON THINLY SLICED FRESH SAGE

2 TEASPOONS UNSALTED BUTTER, AT ROOM TEMPERATURE

SEA SALT AND FRESHLY GROUND BLACK PEPPER

Heat the oil in a heavy skillet over medium heat. Add the pork belly. Cook for 3 to 4 minutes, or until the pieces begin to brown. Add the shallots and cook for about 5 minutes, or until softened and nicely browned and caramelized.

With a slotted spoon, transfer the pork belly and shallots to a warm plate lined with a clean kitchen towel to drain.

Remove about half of the fat from the skillet. Add the mushrooms and cook, covered, for about 2 minutes over high heat, or until the pan fills with liquid exuded by the mushrooms. Uncover the pan and cook for about 1 minute longer, or until the liquid evaporates.

Return the pork belly and shallots to the skillet and cook for about 1 minute longer. Stir in the sage and butter. Season to taste with salt and pepper. Serve immediately.

APPLE-ROSEMARY PUREE

Whenever I bring up apple-rosemary puree, I am questioned as to the sense of it. This happens even with fellow chefs, and my response to them and anyone else is, "You'll see!" I don't say more because it's so much fun to witness the expression on their faces when they taste the puree for the first time. Apples and rosemary are remarkable together, particularly if you pair the puree with any kind of protein. Your first thoughts probably would be to serve it with pork or chicken, but I especially like the puree with fish. We serve it with Seared Trout (page 134) and it's also astonishing with sea scallops, monkfish, barramundi, or any seafood you can imagine.

Serves 4

6 TART HEIRLOOM APPLES, SUCH AS COX'S ORANGE PIPPIN, NEWTOWN PIPPIN, ROXBURY RUSSET, AND REAL GRANNY SMITHS, PEELED, CORED, AND SLICED

2 CUPS MILK

2 CUPS WATER

1 LARGE ROSEMARY SPRIG

4 TABLESPOONS UNSALTED BUTTER, SOFTENED

2 TEASPOONS SEA SALT

FRESHLY GROUND BLACK PEPPER

Bring the apples, milk, water, and rosemary to a slow simmer in a saucepan over medium-low heat. Cook for about 10 minutes, or until the apples soften but are not mushy.

Drain the apples through a colander, reserving the cooking liquid. Set aside for at least 10 minutes to ensure that the apples drain completely.

Discard the rosemary. Transfer the apples to a blender. Add the butter. Puree until smooth. Add some of the reserved cooking liquid, if necessary, to thin out the puree. Season to taste with salt and pepper. Set aside, covered, to keep warm until ready to serve.

SPICY EGGPLANT

Imagine all the great flavors of ratatouille but with vibrant color and great texture (ratatouille is by design cooked until very soft). I especially like this spicy dish served alongside meat and poultry. I also appreciate its healthfulness, provided in great measure by the dark, nutrient-rich kale. What a tasty way to get more dark, leafy greens into your diet. The chile peppers are included for their spiciness as well as their vitamin C. One cherry pepper has the vitamin C of 10 oranges!

Makes about 2 quarts

3 RED, YELLOW, OR ORANGE BELL PEPPERS OR A MIXTURE
    OF THESE COLORS, SEEDED AND MEMBRANES DISCARDED

1 JALAPEÑO CHILE PEPPER, SEEDED (WEAR PLASTIC GLOVES
    WHEN HANDLING)

1 HOT RED CHERRY PEPPER, SEEDED (WEAR PLASTIC GLOVES
    WHEN HANDLING)

1 LARGE TOMATO, HALVED

1 RED ONION

1 Black Beauty EGGPLANT

1 SMALL WHITE ASIAN EGGPLANT

$1/4$ CUP OLIVE OIL

2 CUPS CHOPPED KALE (ABOUT 2 LARGE LEAVES, RIBS TRIMMED)

KOSHER SALT AND FRESHLY GROUND BLACK PEPPER

FINELY GRATED ZEST AND JUICE OF 1 LEMON

Julienne the bell peppers, chile pepper, and cherry pepper. Cut the tomato halves into $1/2$" cubes. Slice the onion into $1/4$"-thick slices. Peel and cube the Black Beauty eggplant into large cubes, about $1\frac{1}{2}$" wide. Peel and slice the Asian eggplant into rounds.

Heat the oil in a large skillet or wide, deep pot over medium heat. Add the onion and eggplant. Cook for about 5 minutes, tossing 2 or 3 times to coat well with oil. Add the kale. Season to taste with salt and pepper. Increase the heat to medium-high. Cover and cook for 8 to 10 minutes, or until the eggplant begins to brown.

Add the peppers, tomato, lemon zest, and lemon juice. Cook for 2 to 4 minutes longer, or until the flavors blend and the mixture is fragrant. Season to taste with salt and pepper. Serve immediately.

PEACH *and* FENNEL SLAW

When you want a side with more texture and weight than a typical lettuce salad, try this incredible fennel slaw made with summer's freshest, juiciest peaches. You can use any other stone fruit with the fennel, which provides the crunch of cabbage but has a seductive anise flavor. Serve this alongside any summer meal of grilled meats, or pile it on sandwiches. Between this and the Apple Slaw on page 226, you have nearly a half year—or 2 full seasons—of slaw!

Serves 4 or 5

2 FENNEL BULBS

2 TABLESPOONS RIESLING WINE VINEGAR OR OTHER
   WHITE WINE VINEGAR

KOSHER SALT

2 RIPE PEACHES, HALVED AND PITS REMOVED

2 TABLESPOONS FLAT-LEAF PARSLEY

1 TABLESPOON FRESH TARRAGON

1 TABLESPOON FRESHLY GRATED LEMON ZEST

FRESHLY GROUND BLACK PEPPER

Remove the fennel fronds. Chop enough of the fronds to equal ¼ cup and set aside. Discard the stalks.

Quarter the fennel bulbs lengthwise. Remove the cores from each quarter so that the fennel layers are free of each other.

Put the fennel quarters in a large mixing bowl. Add the vinegar and a little salt. Let stand for 10 to 15 minutes, or until the fennel has softened slightly.

Cut the peach halves into ⅛"-thick slices. Add to the mixing bowl. Add the parsley, tarragon, lemon zest, and reserved chopped fennel fronds. Toss very gently so as not to break up the peach slices. Season to taste with salt and pepper and serve.

APPLE SLAW

Savoy cabbage has a nuttiness that goes beautifully with the apples in this slaw, which makes it perfect for the late summer and early fall to serve with ribs, grilled sausage, or anything you fancy. It's especially good with fresh apples from your local farmers' market.

Serves 4 or 5

1/4 POUND SAVOY CABBAGE, LEAVES SEPARATED, LARGE RIBS REMOVED

3 TABLESPOONS GOOD RIESLING VINEGAR OR OTHER WHITE WINE VINEGAR

KOSHER SALT

2 TART HEIRLOOM APPLES, THE CRISPER THE BETTER

1/4 CUP FRESHLY PICKED CHERVIL

FRESHLY GROUND BLACK PEPPER

Stack the cabbage leaves in piles as thick as you can handle. Slice the cabbage leaves into thin shreds for coleslaw with a large chef's knife.

Put the shreds in a large mixing bowl. Toss with 2 tablespoons of the vinegar and a little salt. Set aside for about 10 minutes, or until the cabbage begins to soften and weep. Drain the cabbage by holding on to it as you tilt the bowl over the sink. You do not need to remove all the liquid. *Do not* squeeze the cabbage.

Core the apples and cut into wedges. Slice the wedges into thin pieces and add to the cabbage. Add the chervil and remaining 1 tablespoon of vinegar. Toss well. Season to taste with salt and pepper.

RESOURCES

If you want to read more, below are some helpful Web sites to inform and help you as you try to live, cook, and eat more sustainably.

GENERAL INFORMATION ON SUSTAINABILITY

HTTP://ATTRA.NCAT.ORG
WWW.AUDUBON.ORG
HTTP://CHGE.MED.HARVARD.EDU
WWW.EWG.ORG
WWW.EDF.ORG
WWW.FARMLAND.ORG
WWW.HSPH.HARVARD.EDU
WWW.LEOPOLD.IASTATE.EDU
WWW.NRDC.ORG
WWW.SAREP.UCDAVIS.EDU

HEIRLOOM GRAINS, GRITS, AND GRINDING CORN

WWW.ANSONMILLS.COM
WWW.HOMEGROWNHARVEST.COM
WWW.INDIANHARVEST.COM

SEAFOOD CHOICES

WWW.BLUEOCEAN.ORG
WWW.KIDSAFESEAFOOD.ORG
WWW.MONTEREYBAYAQUARIUM.ORG
WWW.NMFS.NOAA.GOV/FISHWATCH
WWW.PASSIONFISH.NET/
    SUSTAINABLE.HTML
WWW.WORLDWATCH.ORG

BEEF, PORK, LAMB, AND POULTRY CHOICES

WWW.HERITAGEFOODSUSA.COM
WWW.NIMANRANCH.COM
WWW.ORGANICCONSUMERS.ORG
WWW.SEARCHORGANIC.COM
WWW.SLOWFOODUSA.ORG

FARMERS' MARKETS

WWW.100MILEDIET.ORG
WWW.AMS.USDA.GOV/AMSv1.0
WWW.LOCALHARVEST.ORG
WWW.WHOLESOMEWAVE.ORG

A SUSTAINABLE KITCHEN

My dear friend Renée Loux, author of *Easy Green Living,* has assembled a list of useful Web sites and a few products for my readers that will help in your journey to living sustainably. I thank her from the bottom of my heart for this help.

ECO CHOICES ECO KITCHEN

WWW.ECOKITCHEN.COM/
    GREEN HOME GUIDE—KNOW HOW,
    KITCHENS
WWW.GREENHOMEGUIDE.COM
GREEN KITCHEN DESIGN GUIDE
    WWW.GREENKITCHENDESIGNGUIDE.
    COM
PLANET GREEN—HOW TO GO
    GREEN: IN THE KITCHEN
    HTTP://PLANETGREEN.DISCOVERY.
    COM/GO-GREEN/KITCHEN/

Green Kitchen Cleaning

Caldrea—liquid dish soap, auto dish detergent, APC, counter cleaner, glass cleaner, surface scrub, stainless steel cleaner
www.caldrea.com

Earth-Friendly Products—liquid dish soap, auto dish detergent, APC, glass cleaner

Ecover

Method Home—liquid dish soap, auto dish detergent, APC, glass cleaner, surface scrub, stainless steel cleaner

Mrs. Meyers—liquid dish soap, auto dish detergent, APC, counter cleaner, glass cleaner, surface scrub, stainless steel cleaner

Seventh Generation

Green Kitchen Accoutrements, Bamboo Cutting Boards, et al.

Crate & Barrel
www.crateandbarrel.com

Miu France
www.miufrance.com

Sur La Table
www.surlatable.com

Totally Bamboo
www.totallybamboo.com

Whole Foods
www.wholefoodsmarket.com

Williams and Sonoma
www.williams-sonoma.com

Cookware

Enameled Cast Iron

Chantal
www.chantal.com

Kintec
www.innova-inc.com

Le Crueset
www.lecreuset.com

Staub
www.staubusa.com

Cast Iron

Iittala Hackman
www.iittala.com

Lodge Manufacturing
www.lodgemfg.com

Glass and Ceramic

Corningware
www.corningware.com

KitchenAid
www.kitchenaid.com

Luminarc
www.luminarc.us

ACKNOWLEDGMENTS

Thanks to:

Rodale, for publishing *Sustainably Delicious* and welcoming me with such enthusiasm and support. We are "on the same page," and for that I am particularly appreciative. I am grateful finally to have the opportunity to work with Pam Krauss, whose editorial talents challenged my creativity in a way that has made this far more than just a cookbook.

Mary Goodbody and I have been writing together for some time now, and it's difficult to know just where my thoughts begin and hers end—a good thing when you're writing books together. Her common sense and dedication to the things we both believe in helped turn over quite a few stones along the way. If not for her diligence, you would not be reading this book.

Lori, my beautiful wife of 25 years who keeps our family and garden growing in ways that often defy common rationale or logic. Everything in our relationship is unconditional. I love her.

My amazing children—each and every one of the five—for providing the diversity in life that only a family of completely independent/interdependent beings can provide. The result is a true understanding that love and thankfulness surely win over anger and frustration. They are me and I am them, whether we like it or not!

Paul Newman, who would say the quality of his public incarnation and his private self were made possible mostly by the undeniable influence of his beloved wife and partner, Joanne Woodward. The rest of his family would echo the sentiment. Joanne is indeed one of the kindest, purest, most gracefully significant and courageous humans my family and I have had the privilege of knowing. Her wisdom and influence are at once subtle and profound—no doubt about it.

Nell Newman, for being the tireless, stubborn (like her pop) advocate and endlessly faithful person she is, and for introducing me to her amazingly diverse and wonderful family. Our friendship and warm encounters have only grown and galvanized the work we do in both the for-profit and not-for-profit worlds. Nell is not just a good egg, she's the best egg—or should I say peach? She is fiercely sweet, bright as the sun, and relentless as a bear who knows there's honey stuck in that there petrified stump. She will never give up, and we'll all be better for it.

Those chefs who are true pioneers, friends, and inspirations—all of whose apron strings I am unfit to tie. They've worked far and away harder than the average chef to fight for and run successful businesses while buying and cooking great food from local, organic, sustainable sources—far more difficult to obtain and way more expensive than food from the conventional system. They are:

Dan Barber, Rick Bayless, Kathleen Blake, Jimmy Boyce, Joe Bruno, Jesse Cool, Sam Hayward, Greg Higgins, Maria Hines, Peter Hoffman, Linton Hopkins, Melissa Kelly,

Rick Moonen, Odessa Piper, Alain Sailhac, Michael Schwartz, John Sundstrom, Hidekazu Tojo, and Judy Wicks. Thankfully, there are many, many more, but these are a few who I am privileged to know.

Special thanks to Nora Pouillon and Alice Waters. Between the two there is unwavering commitment, a sense of endless possibility, a love of excellence and all things beautiful, and an almost childlike wonderment at how food will always be truly amazing. Alice is relentless in her commitment to bringing her invaluable message and graceful desire to see the world become a more deliciously beautiful place. Nora, who works in the nation's capital and has been a major player in the sustainable movement for 30 years, has accomplished astonishing food system work in a region with limited space and a 5-month growing season. Her humility has often caused her work to be less noticed and celebrated than it should be, but its grace creates the reality of Nora—committed, sincere, and undeniably significant to the cause.

Special thanks to Jacques Pepin, who along with Julia Child convinced Americans that being able to cook well is a very wonderful and necessary thing. Jacques has helped save us from our convenience-minded selves and created an environment in which aspiring chefs can flourish. I regard him as a true culinary forefather for the gentle and hands-on way he constantly encourages me and all chefs, aspiring and accomplished, to consider the impact of every decision we make and every word we say. He understands the influence of chefs on the world and strives to see that the net effect is positive, wonderful, and delicious. He is the culinary Dalai Lama.

Shep Gordon, who has been one of my finest, most highly valued mentors in life. While many are mentors for a short period, Shep holds a position of rare permanence. He is a friend who helps steward the journey of life rather than a craft, art, or business. His calm constancy serves as a submerged rudder that holds steady, no matter where either of us might be at a given time. A very good man indeed,

Renée Loux, whose jubilance, joy in the cause, and willingness to share are hard for anyone to match. As a friend, she offers a unique brand of optimism and hope for ideas that, by nature, expose truths that are difficult for humans to face. As a colleague, she offers undying support, contacts, ideas, and information with open generosity.

Oran Hesterman, who has taught me to mine very deeply to expose the direct and inseparable connection between food and society. His work and unstoppable commitment to make this connection possible for all humans is extraordinary. He is not white, black, native, or imported. He is a pure human of all colors and creeds, and I am humbled to call him my friend.

I am also indebted to Debi Callen, whose help testing the recipes allows me to sleep at night, knowing that each and every one is completely trustworthy in a home kitchen.

I also want to thank Johnny Holzwarth and John Vaast from Dressing Room. Their help during the process of writing the book and their dedication to sustainability remains an invaluable part of Dressing Room's magic. It is very special to have a chef and sous chef who can work in collaboration around the shared cause of making the world a more sustainably delicious place to live.

Farmers, who are the "first chefs" of all good food, deserve gratitude and support from us all. I would like to mention:

Fred Kirschenmann, who is director emeritus of the Leopold Center for Sustainable Agriculture and organic farming pioneer/advocate, has provided me and many chefs with incredible insight, friendship, data, truth, encouragement, and challenging calls to process our thoughts in ways we might never have imagined on our own. He is simply brilliant—and great to share a beer with.

Annie Farrell, who is one of the most tireless, energetic, gregarious, and generous farming pioneers any chef could meet. Her commitment not only to sustainability but also to drawing everyone she encounters into the act of it is unmatched by almost anyone I know. She also has a somewhat skewed sense of time. If you ever have the privilege of meeting her and she invites you for a short tour of Millstone Farm, make sure you have a couple of hours on your hands. I promise every second will be worth it.

Betsy Fink, who owns Millstone Farm, is a board member of Wholesome Wave Foundation. Her embrace of farming, the issue of climate change, humanities, and all their interrelations is more than inspiring. She also possesses a secret weapon in the form of her husband, Jesse. Their work through MissionPoint Capital, Millstone Farm, and Marshall Street Management will help change the world. Their support has informed my course greatly.

Gus Schumacher, who is the chairman of Wholesome Wave Foundation, is a farmer, former undersecretary of Agriculture for the US Department of Agriculture, commissioner of agriculture for the state of Massachusetts, statesman, advocate, peacemaker, and innovator who absolutely refuses to take credit for the many amazing things he quietly accomplishes. I am not alone in my belief that he is responsible for forming food policy that allowed the use of food stamps and WIC coupons at farmers' markets. His respect for seniors resulted in the Seniors Farmers' Market Nutrition Program, making federal funds available to bolster this population's buying power at local farm stands. A conversation he and I once had, which he largely led, resulted in an idea to double the value of food stamps and other government-issued, hunger-relief benefits to support the health of both people from historically excluded communities and farmers. What was largely his idea became, at Gus's insistence, my idea. However hard I try, I cannot persuade him to take or share any credit for what could very well become a life-altering innovation for our food system. His hard work and humility are a fine example indeed.

Finally, to all of those people and things—living or otherwise—for whom and which I am eternally grateful, for they all have contributed to my life in ways that have resulted in this book: potato beetles, squash vine borers, and woodchucks—their skills of evasion and their occasional capture—hummingbirds, deer fencing, weeds of all kinds, bean inoculants, blisters, Native American activists and farmers, blackberry thorns, flea beetles, bailing twine, earthworms, sunburn, compost, errant teens, wondrously curious toddlers, drought, hail, hay forks, sunshine, my fire pit, butterflies, deer in the early evening (outside my deer fence), augers, fireflies, slugs, rocks, cold beer, chicken manure, Lori's company by the fire in the midst of the garden, and so much more.

INDEX

Underscored page references indicate boxed text or cook's notes. **Boldfaced** page references indicate photographs.